Answers
for Atheists, Agnostics,
and Other Thoughtful Skeptics

Also by E. Calvin Beisner

God in Three Persons
(Tyndale House, 1984)
New Testament evidence for the doctrine of the Trinity, description of the
early development of the doctrine, and comparison of the doctrine in the
Nicene Creed and the Bible.

*Prosperity and Poverty: The Compassionate Use of Resources in a World
of Scarcity*
(Crossway Books, 1988)
An introduction to economics, the economic role of the state, and help for the
poor from the perspective of Biblical ethics and theology.

Psalms of Promise: Exploring the Majesty and Faithfulness of God
(NavPress, 1988; currently available only from the author)
A study of the theme of the covenant in nineteen selected Psalms, arranged by
subject from creation to consummation, focusing on the believer's privileges
and duties in relationship with God.

*Prospects for Growth: A Biblical View of Population, Resources, and
the Future*
(Crossway Books, 1990)
Biblical and empirical demonstration that population growth is a blessing, not
a curse, that human creativity, reflecting the image of God, increases resources
over time, and that economic growth and Christian stewardship can improve
the world's environment.

Answers for Atheists, Agnostics, and Other Thoughtful Skeptics

Dialogs About Christian Faith and Life

Revised Edition

E. Calvin Beisner

CROSSWAY BOOKS • WHEATON, ILLINOIS
A DIVISION OF GOOD NEWS PUBLISHERS

E. Calvin Beisner, *Answers for Atheists, Agnostics, and Other Thoughtful Skeptics: Dialogs About Christian Faith and Life*

Foreign language editions, copyright © 1985 by Campus Crusade for Christ, International.

English language edition, copyright © 1985

Revised edition, copyright © 1993 by E. Calvin Beisner. Published by Crossway Books, 1300 Crescent Street, Wheaton, IL 60187.

Cover design: Russ Peterson

First printing, in Russian, 1985

First printing, in English, 1985

First printing, in Estonian, 1989

First printing, revised English edition, 1993.

Unless otherwise indicated, Scripture quotations are taken from the *New King James Version*, © 1988, Thomas Nelson, Inc.

Library of Congress Cataloging-in-Publication Data
Beisner, E. Calvin.
    Answers for atheists, agnostics, and other thoughtful skeptics :
dialogs about Christian faith and life / E. Calvin Beisner. — Rev.
English ed.
        p.   cm.
    Includes bibliographical references.
    1. Apologetics—20th century.   I. Title.
BT1102.B335 1992   239'.7—dc20   92-41614
ISBN 0-89107-700-6

01	00	99	98	97	96	95	94	93
15	14	13	12	11	10	9	8	7	6	5	4	3	2	1

To Rebekah,
whose loving spirit
is a testimony of the
grace of God

Contents

evil? Is moral freedom a sufficient answer to the problem of evil? What good is evil? Does the end justify the means? What is moral freedom? Is God morally free? Is man morally free? What is God's highest goal in creating the world? What difference does it make whether our view of the world is God-centered or man-centered? How does evil display the perfection of God? Why was Christ's sacrifice necessary?

reject Christianity? Can anyone who believes in Jesus just go on living as he pleases? Can God forgive really terrible sins?

Acknowledgments

Sixteen apologists, past and present, have profoundly shaped my understanding of the defense of the Christian faith. These men of God have, through their writings and, in some instances, their personal friendships, given me sound examples, reliable information and arguments, and high standards toward which to aim. I am painfully aware that any one of them could have done better than I have done here, but this book may perhaps still be of value to those honestly seeking reasons for the Christian faith, whether Christians or non-Christians. This book is dedicated, therefore, to:

St. Athanasius of Alexandria
Reverend Alexander Balmain Bruce
James Oliver Buswell, Jr.
Bishop Joseph Butler
Norman L. Geisler
Carl F. H. Henry
C. S. Lewis
John Warwick Montgomery
William Paley
Bob and Gretchen Passantino
Francis A. Schaeffer
R. C. Sproul
St. Thomas Aquinas
Benjamin Breckinridge Warfield
Dallas Willard

Foreword

By Dan Griswold

Cal Beisner and I first met over lunch several years ago on a sunny spring day in Colorado. I was a nonbeliever at the time, and I casually mentioned to Cal in the parking lot afterwards that I wanted to learn more about the Bible. What followed was a textbook example of friendship evangelism.

We played tennis together. We talked politics. We discussed books. That fall my wife, Elizabeth, and I joined a weekly Bible study Cal had begun to lead. And I began to question Cal about his evident faith.

"What about those people, living in a jungle somewhere, who never get to hear about Jesus?" I asked. Or, "Does a true Christian need to be a pacifist? After, all, didn't Jesus say to turn the other cheek?" "Isn't the Biblical story of creation awfully unscientific?" "Why do we need Jesus? Can't we just pray directly to God?" And so on.

Patiently, with obvious love and respect, Cal did his best to give me answers. If he didn't have an immediate response, he said he would research it and get back to me. And he always did. He even sought my input on a passage for a small book he was writing at the time. The book was to be a dialog between a believer and a skeptic.

Cal and his young family left Colorado Springs before my wife and I became believers. But he had laid the groundwork. In witnessing to me, he had appealed to my reason, not just my heart. He had made Christianity intellectually respectable.

Only God can move a man's heart to follow Jesus Christ as Lord and Savior. But that does not mean Christianity is exclusively an experience of the heart. Some of the best minds of the last 2,000 years, from the Apostle Paul to Thomas Aquinas to Martin Luther and John Calvin, have spent their lives contemplating the mysteries of God's provision for believers through His Son, Jesus Christ.

This book is written for those people who, like me that spring day years ago, are looking for answers to life's deepest questions and are willing to listen to the witness of a learned believer. Cal Beisner would be the first to acknowledge that this book does not contain all the answers. But it will help to clear away the intellectual underbrush that may stand between a skeptical inquirer and the only knowledge that really counts in life—knowing the Lord Jesus Christ and being known by Him.

—Dan Griswold
Editorial page editor,
Colorado Springs *Gazette-Telegraph*
August 31, 1992
Colorado Springs, Colorado

Preface

to the Revised Edition

When asked in 1984 by Campus Crusade for Christ's covert evangelistic mission to the former Soviet Union to write a simple book of questions and answers on reasons for Christian faith, I could hardly have dreamed the extent to which that book would be used. The idea was simply to provide a book that non-specialists in apologetics would find helpful in witnessing to people with little or no prior acquaintance with Christianity. Publication was planned only in Russian, and distribution would be almost solely person-to-person in Russia.

Instead, word got around among American staff of Campus Crusade for Christ that the little book was an effective apologetics/evangelism training tool, and they began requesting it in English. So a small division of Crusade produced a single printing in a cheap format, and distribution continued largely through Crusade's training channels, supplemented slightly by my personal sales. Many users—and the book is meant to be used, not merely read—have reported finding the book helpful.

Just when copies of the English edition were running out,

requests for the book multiplied. At the same time, I had been praying for an opportunity to revise the book—to make it more interesting to read and to improve some of the arguments in it. But by then the Crusade division had moved—lock, stock, and barrel—to Moscow, and producing a new English edition, or even reprinting the original, would have been financially unfeasible. Much to my delight, Jan Dennis, then with Crossway Books, saw potential for the book and agreed to publish a new edition. This is the result.

The book is meant to provide clear and fairly simple—but not simplistic—answers to a wide variety of questions frequently posed by thoughtful nonbelievers about Christianity. Readers should entertain no illusions about arguing anyone to faith. That cannot be done. The proper role of apologetics is not to push people down the road to the cross but to fill in potholes and remove barriers along it. Only the Spirit of God can draw people to Christ, and their coming requires His supernatural, miraculous work in their hearts, making blind eyes see and deaf ears hear and dark minds bright and cold hearts warm. That is why effective apologetic evangelism requires constant prayer for the hearers.

I have tried here to avoid two temptations common to many efforts in apologetics and evangelism.

First, the temptation to oversimplify and minimize the seriousness of intellectual objections to faith—particularly, to assume too quickly that someone's intellectual objection is a mere mask for moral rebellion. Often people do hide behind intellectual questions, but if they are to be made aware that those objections are inadequate hiding-places, the objections must be answered fairly and fully. Often, too, people point out real weaknesses in Christian thought and practice. Rather than ignoring or minimizing those, we need to confront them boldly, correct our thinking where it is wrong (as I have sought to do by several changes in this book), and admit our failures in practice. We are, after all, followers of One who said He came to save sinners, not the "righteous."

Second, the temptation to minimize the demands of the gospel on the unconverted. The common idea that one can receive Christ as Savior without submitting to Him as Lord lies at the root, I believe, of the ineffectiveness of much contemporary "Christianity" in the West. Ours has become a church of the unconverted, happily assured (they think) of their reconciliation with God but differing little or not at all from the unreconciled world about them. Make no mistake about it: saving grace is transforming grace; justification must bear fruit in sanctification; there is no pardon without repentance; Jesus Christ's saving work is inseparable from His Lordship. Authentic evangelism insists that those who come to Christ come not only for forgiveness but also to have their lives transformed. We need not fear that we will reap smaller harvests because we preach this whole gospel. On the contrary, many people will respond to this message gladly who would never respond to the counterfeit "just receive Jesus and live as you please" gospel. They know the disappointments and tragedies of living in sin. They know they are slaves to sin. They are looking for liberation, and only the real gospel can offer it. And when these people come to Christ, they will turn around and bear fruit themselves, multiplying the impact of our preaching.

May this new edition bear fruit to the glory and praise of God, who alone is worthy to be praised!

August 31, 1992

Introduction

If you're like most Christians who have witnessed more than a few times to others about Christ, you have probably experienced meeting someone with honest, sincere interest in the Christian faith—someone whose conversation indicates that he is not just playing games with you, but who also has some very difficult questions he wants answered before he decides how to respond to Christ. Often these questions concern matters that would be difficult to answer in a short time, and sometimes they cover such a broad range of subjects that it seems impossible for any one Christian to answer them all with confidence without being a specialist in apologetics—giving reasons for the faith.

If this situation seems familiar, or if you expect to meet such people in the future, or even if you simply have questions of your own about reasons for the Christian faith, this book is for you. It offers clear, reasonably simple answers to some of the more difficult questions Christians often face about their faith. One thing makes it significantly different from nearly every other book of its kind: it does *not* assume that either the

Christian or the non-Christian already has a broad and intricate grasp of technical terms in Christian thought. The book was written so it could be used in communicating the gospel effectively even with someone who has never before had any contact with Christianity—who has never heard of Jesus Christ, who has never heard of the Bible, and who would be mystified if he heard a Christian start right out talking about sin, sacrifice, redemption, justification, the cross, atonement, the incarnation, or any other such thing. This means you will find here a gradual, step-by-step unfolding of the basic points of the Christian faith, with each new point defined as it comes up so everything is clear from start to finish.

The book is in dialog form—a Christian, Jim, speaking with his non-Christian friend, Dave. The dialog picks up after Jim has introduced Dave to the idea of God. Dave responds that he believes—as modern science makes clear, of course!—that only matter and energy are real. From there, they exchange ideas and the conversation proceeds in logical order from the reality of non-material things through the reality of God, the sinfulness of man, the incarnation and atoning death of Christ, the deity of Christ, the way of salvation, and finally a clear invitation to repent of sin and trust in Jesus Christ as Lord and Savior. Along the way, as in all natural conversations, there are excursions into important side issues: Why is there evil if God is all-good and all-powerful? If Christianity is so great, why are there so few Christians? What about those who never hear the gospel? Is the Bible reliable? What about evolution? Why should I believe in Christ when Christianity has done so many awful things in the past?

The best way to use this book is to internalize the reasons for faith given here so much that you can pass them along to others who ask about them without needing to refer again to the book. You might also consider asking a non-Christian friend to read through the book and discuss it with you later.

Or you might use the book as a stepping-off point for you to learn much more about apologetics by reading some of the books cited in the notes and recommended at the end.

I pray that you will find this book helpful in your own thinking and as you share the wonderful gospel of Jesus Christ with others. And if you are a non-Christian reading this, I pray that through it you will come to know Christ, to be convinced of the truth of the Christian faith, and to know the joy of being made right with God.

Many thanks to Campus Crusade for Christ, International, for giving me the idea for the original edition of this book, requesting that I write it for translation and use in Russian, and providing some of the raw material that went into it. May the Lord greatly enrich that ministry as it reaches out to those imprisoned in darkness—in more ways than one.

In Christ's joyous service,
E. Calvin Beisner
August 31, 1992
Soli Deo Gloria!

Chapter 1

Is There
a God?

Jim Edwards and Dave Wright had been friends for a little
over two years. They had met in a graduate philosophy class
and found they had lots in common—hang gliding, tennis, and
techno-thriller novels among them.

They also both loved a good argument. Neither was
offended, so long as the argument stayed on the issues and
didn't become a personal attack. And both were good at stick-
ing with the issues.

What divided them was that Jim was a Christian and
Dave wasn't. Far from it! Dave—who had been a physics
major in undergraduate school—was a convinced atheist, a
materialist in fact. For him, nothing but matter and energy
existed. Science provided—or would provide—explanations
for everything, and sound philosophy agreed. To Dave, Jim's
beliefs were, well, irrational, to put it politely.

Jim, of course, thought otherwise. To him, the God of the
Bible was the bedrock on which all other rationality stood.
Apart from God, nothing made any sense at all. Not the sci-

ence Dave held so dear, not the philosophy they both enjoyed, nothing.

Each was dedicated to his view. But each was dedicated to the other, too. They valued their friendship; they studied and played together whenever they could. That's where things stood one day when they got together in the library, as they often did, to study and, for some relief, debate with each other.

"Sorry, Jim, but I just can't take this God business seriously," Dave said. "I simply know no good reason to believe that anything other than matter and energy is real. Empiricism—that's the philosophy for me. Give me something I can grasp with my senses, something I can quantify, something I can examine. Your talk about God is just so much gibberish so far as I'm concerned. It doesn't mean anything."

Jim thought for a minute. Dave had invited several avenues of attack. His forthright assertion of empiricism was surprising, granted the beating empiricism had taken in philosophical circles over the last half century. He ought to know that. Hadn't he taken the history of modern philosophy? Then again, Dave had said merely that he knew no good reason to believe anything but matter and energy existed. That left the door wide open. *I'll offer him a good reason,* Jim thought.

"You're really sure of that, are you, Dave? There's no good reason to believe in anything but matter and energy?"

"Of course I'm sure."

"Well," Jim said, "I can give you not only a good reason to believe, but solid proof that matter and energy aren't the only things that exist."

"How?"

"Matter and energy have no ordering, or organizing, principle in themselves. Left to themselves, they would never have produced the order around us, and left to themselves even now they would eventually reach the point of absolute disorder—maximum randomness, I think it's called."

"You're talking about the principle of entropy," Dave said.

"Right. You're the physics buff. The Second Law of Thermodynamics. All matter and energy tends toward maximum randomness; available energy in any closed system decreases through time."

"Sure," Dave said. "Everybody knows that. It's what leads scientists like Isaac Asimov to predict that the universe, eventually, will reach the point of 'heat death,' when all available energy will have been used up, all order in the universe will cease, and everything—biological and mechanical—will grind to a halt. So what?"

"Two things, Dave. First, since matter and energy don't have an ordering principle inherent in themselves, but rather a disordering principle, without something other than matter and energy to enforce order on them, there could be no order or design in the universe. Everything would be absolutely random. There would be no thinking and nothing to think about. You and I wouldn't be talking here."

"Nonsense, Jim. Some matter does impose order on other matter. Your genes caused the order of your body, for instance."

"But genes only order other things because they themselves are first ordered. That doesn't explain anything, Dave. It just pushes the answer back a step. Whatever little bits of order and of order-causing matter there may be in the universe, genes included, can't have caused their own order. And the universe as a whole can't have brought about that order either, if the universe is entirely material. So there must be a cause for order outside the universe.

"But second, since all matter and energy tend irreversibly toward maximum randomness, and since the universe is not maximally random today, it cannot have been tending that direction forever. This means that matter and energy aren't eternal; there was a time when they didn't exist. So, since nothing comes from nothing, something other than matter and energy must have existed before matter and energy."

"Run that by me again?"

"Sure. We're really left with only two options. Either we believe nothing exists, or we believe matter and energy *and something else* exist. Because believing that only matter and energy exist means denying the Second Law of Thermodynamics."

"I see where you're headed," Dave said. "If entropy has been in force as long as matter and energy have existed, and matter and energy aren't now in a state of maximum entropy—maximum randomness, or heat death—then entropy can't have been operating forever."

"Exactly. In which case," Jim concluded, "matter and energy haven't been around forever, and since they can't have come from nothing, they must have come from something other than matter and energy. So matter and energy aren't the only things that exist."

"Okay," Dave said. "I'll concede the point—for the sake of argument, anyway. But that doesn't exactly give you God. We might know that something other than matter and energy exists, but we can't really know anything about it. After all, statements only mean something if they can be investigated for truth or falsehood by empirical means."

"You're talking about the verifiability principle," said Jim. "I figured that was coming, since you called yourself an empiricist a while back."

"Right. That's the scientific approach. Nothing is verifiable that can't be tested empirically."

"Including that principle itself?" Jim asked.

"Of course."

"Fine. Verify the principle of verifiability for me empirically. Give me empirical evidence for it."

"Huh?"

"Put the principle to its own test."

"Well, it's what every scientist assumes. You just don't bother with things that aren't subject to some kind of empirical verification."

"Every scientist, Dave?"

"Sure."

"What about Robert Jastrow, the astrophysicist?"

"What about him?"

"He's a scientist, isn't he?"

"Of course."

"Well, he's one scientist who isn't an empiricist. And he doesn't believe only matter and energy are real either."

"Where'd you hear that?"

"I didn't hear it, Dave. I read it, in his book *God and the Astronomers*. You ought to read it. It's fascinating. In one part of it, he says he's an agnostic, but he adds that recent developments in astronomy have proved conclusively that the universe was created. And he chides other astronomers for getting irritated at that conclusion, a conclusion brought about by the evidence they themselves uncovered through their empirical research."[1]

"Interesting. But you're changing the subject. You're talking about creation, and we were talking about empiricism and the principle that nothing is meaningful that can't be verified or falsified by empirical evidence."

"They're all connected, Dave. Don't you see it? Empiricism is only true if only matter and energy are real, and matter and energy can't be the only real things if something existed before them and brought them into existence. So the creation of matter and energy disproves materialism, and if materialism is false, empiricism must be false, too."

"A plausible line of argument. But I'm not convinced. Science has gone a long way on empiricism."

"No, Dave, it hasn't. Science does great so long as it deals only with empirical questions, the day-to-day questions of science. But it can't deal with a more fundamental question that way."

"What question is that?"

"The very nature of science. What science is, what it does, and why.[2] Why, after all, do scientists believe that empirical evidence is worth anything?"

"Because they've tested it over and over and found it reliable."

"Reliable within its boundaries, yes. But they can't give empirical evidence for their belief in the reliability of empirical evidence. If they did, they'd be—"

"Arguing in a circle. I see the point."

"Look, Dave, empirical evidence is fine so long as you're dealing only with empirical realities, as science normally does. But when you start dealing with non-empirical realities— things that are neither matter nor energy—empirical evidence is utterly inadequate. And that's precisely why the basic principle of empiricism, that a statement is meaningful only if it is empirically verifiable, is nonsense."

"What do you mean?"

"It doesn't stand up to its own test. You can't give any empirical evidence for it, because it isn't a statement about empirical things. It's a statement about ultimate reality and ultimate truth, and it isn't open to any kind of empirical testing. But since it says only statements open to empirical testing are sensible, and it isn't open to empirical testing, it's nonsense. It's self-defeating."

Dave could see the handwriting on the wall. He was trapped. And he was honest enough to admit it. But he wasn't going to give away any more than was absolutely necessary.

"Okay," he conceded. "But that doesn't mean you can actually *know* anything about immaterial things. There just isn't any method by which to know anything about them. The whole idea is utterly unscientific."

"You sure of that, Dave?"

"Sure, I'm sure."

"Sure you can't know anything about immaterial things?"

"Yeah."

"And you know that?" Jim laughed.

Dave paused. *I should have seen that coming*, he thought.

"All right, I deserved that."

"You sure did," Jim said. "But I won't rub it in."

"Not much!" Dave said. He knew Jim wouldn't let him forget it.

"So you admit it's possible, at least in theory, to know something about immaterial things?"

"In theory, yes. In practice? I'm from Missouri, Jim. Show me! Aside from the theoretical point that it's possible to know something about immaterial things, I don't think you can know anything else about them."

"Except that you can't know anything else about them?"

Dave laughed at himself this time.

"Caught you again, didn't I? I figured you'd be once burned, twice shy, Dave!"

"Go ahead, rub it in!"

"Why bother? You're doing a good enough job of that yourself," Jim said. "The only logical approach is to admit that you *can* know about immaterial things, and then see where the evidence leads to determine *what* you can know about them."

"So where does it lead?"

"First, we know that they exist—or that at least one immaterial thing exists."

"Fine. That's water under the bridge."

"And we know that at least one immaterial thing created the material universe."

"There you go talking about creation again, Jim. Look, you're going up against the whole scientific world now. Evolution's been tried and tested for over a century."

"Yeah, and so was the idea of a geocentric solar system. Too bad some guy named Copernicus came along and knocked that time-tested scientific theory for a loop."

"But evolution's different. Science was antiquated when people believed the sun revolved around the earth. It's a whole different story now."

"I have a hunch the differences aren't as great as you think they are, but that's beside the point. What's important is that evolution generally doesn't attempt to address the actual origin of the universe. It merely tries to describe how, once the universe existed, things got to be the way they are now. So the idea that something created the universe doesn't really contradict evolution at all."

"Granted. But do *you* believe in evolution yourself?"

"No, but let's not change the subject. We were talking about what we can know about immaterial reality, remember? Not about how you and your dog came to be. We can debate evolution another time."

"So long as you don't avoid the issue."

"I won't, Dave. I won't! But let's try to follow a point through, okay?"

"Sure."

"Okay. We're not talking about how things got to their present form, we're only talking about how the material universe came into existence in the first place."

"If it came into existence at all," said Dave.

"Which you've already admitted," Jim said.

"Well—"

"Or do you want to go back through the Second Law of Thermodynamics again?"

"No. Go ahead. We know the universe had a beginning.

We know there must be at least one immaterial being that created it. But we don't know anything about that being."

"I disagree."

"Figures. So what do you think you know about it?"

"Well, I think we can know that whatever created the universe has more power than all the power in the universe, and that it is intelligent, capable of thinking on levels far beyond our own abilities."

"Hang on a minute. You don't really expect me to buy all that, do you?"

"Not without argument, Dave. I know you too well for that."

"Okay, then, give me some argument."

"Sure. We know that whatever force produces an effect must be sufficient to account for all the force within the effect; an effect cannot be greater than its cause. If an effect were greater than its cause, there would be some part of the effect that was uncaused—that would have come from nothing. But since nothing comes from nothing, no effect can be greater than its cause. So whatever created the material world must be more powerful than the material world.

"Now as for intelligence, matter and energy aren't capable of ordering themselves, right?"

"Right. We've been through that."

"Left to themselves they tend toward maximum disorder. It takes intelligence to bring about order in our material world. When you see a computer, you don't suppose it just happened by accident, you ask who designed it, who built its parts, who put those parts together. When that computer functions, you don't assume it does that by accident either; you ask who wrote the program and who input the data. Right?"

"Sure."

"Well, the universe has much more design than any computer in it. The computer, after all, is part of the universe, and the part can't be greater than the whole. Human brains are thousands of times more complex than any computer, far better designed. The intelligent scientist will ask the same questions about the order in the universe, and the order in the brain, that he asks about the order in the computer: Who designed it? Who gave it the program by which it processes so much information? Who built its parts? Who gave it the energy to function? Unless it designed itself—and you don't suppose it did that, do you?"

"No. Nothing can design itself. That would require its existing before it existed."

"Good. At least we don't have to argue that one through. If it didn't design itself, then its designer must have sufficient intelligence to account for the design within it."

"Fair enough. But that doesn't prove God exists—just that something immaterial exists that created the universe."

"And is extraordinarily powerful and intelligent, right?"

"Right."

"Good. Now, we Christians do believe much *more* than that about God, but we do believe *at least* that. So we're on the way toward Christian belief. You're closer now than you were half an hour ago, right, Dave?"

"I suppose so. But not much."

"Fine. I don't expect to persuade you of much about Christianity in one sitting either. I respect you for how carefully you think things through. But my time's up. I've got to be at work in twenty minutes."

Chapter 2

How Do We Know Things?

The sun beat hot on the sands of Santa Monica Beach. Dave and Jim were stretched out, resting after an hour of body surfing. Their tired muscles needed the break. But their minds were wide awake.

"I've been thinking about our conversation last week, Jim. I'll grant you, materialism can't stand up to scrutiny. But I just don't see how you can really know anything much about God, if He even exists. And I'm not ready to admit that."

"I can understand that, Dave. I'd be surprised if you weren't skeptical. In fact, to some extent anyway I think it's good that you are. Too many people just grab onto the latest silly fad in religion. They don't think carefully. But tell me something, Dave—what would God have to do to prove to you that He exists?"

"What do you mean? I've never thought about that question."

"Well, Dave, when a scientist sets up a hypothesis and attempts to find corroborating or contrary evidence, he usually tries to think of what kinds of evidence would be relevant and convincing in one direction or the other. So, what kinds of evidence would persuade you that God exists?"

"I see what you mean." Dave paused and thought for a minute. He'd never approached questions about God this way. Jim was actually asking him to think about God the way he thought about science.

"Give me a little time, Jim. I'm really not sure what I'd find helpful."

"Let me suggest a few things," Jim said. "You can think about them as we go. If God were to answer a prayer for you, would that help? If He were to become a man and prove Himself through miraculous deeds, through accurate prophecy, and through an exemplary life and teaching that you could explain in no other way, would that be sufficient?"

"I don't know," Dave said. "I'd have to give both of those things a lot of thought. After all, I don't pray—never have. And if I did, how could I be certain that what you'd call an answer to prayer wasn't just coincidence? And the idea that somebody could prove Himself to be God by miracles—I'd find that pretty hard to accept. I don't believe in miracles."

"Fair enough," Jim replied. "But are you at least willing to suspend judgment for a while, to look honestly and carefully at the kinds of evidences I'd like to suggest, before you make up your mind?"

"Sure, Jim. I'll listen."

"Great. One more question: If you were convinced that God exists, would you trust Him? Would you let Him rule your life?"

"Whoa, man! You're pushing too far there. I mean, I suppose I might be willing, but I'd have to see some pretty solid reasons first. What if God exists, but He's evil?"

"Then of course you shouldn't submit to Him. But I think I can show you He's good. If I can, will you submit to Him?"

"If He's really good, maybe. I don't know."

"Fair enough. I can't ask more than that."

Dave was uncomfortable. Jim was getting personal now, and he didn't like it. The earlier discussion had just been theoretical. He could handle that. He didn't like Jim probing this way. He thought it best to turn things back.

"Look, Jim, I really can't tell you what I'd do if you persuaded me that God is real and good. Let's cross that bridge when we come to it—if we ever do. First I want to know if you can give me some really good reasons to believe God exists."

"All right. But let's back up a little first and talk about knowing in general."

"Why go through all that? After all, we've both had epistemology. Can't we just get down to business?"

"Because I want to make sure first that you're willing to apply the same criteria to knowledge about God that you do to other things."

"What do you mean?"

"No double standards. If one kind of evidence is sufficient to persuade you about one thing, it ought to be sufficient to persuade you about other things, too. No special pleading, no fudging around. Okay?"

"I suppose so. But I don't see where this is leading."

"Let me explain." Jim thought to himself for a minute, setting his thoughts in order. He'd point out first the three ways of knowing that he and Dave shared, then dive into the one they didn't.

"It seems to me," Jim said, "that there are three basic ways people know things: reason, experience, and authority. Christians—and many other theists, too—add revelation, which is really just another kind of authority."

"I'm with you on the first three, Jim, but what's revelation?"

"I'll get to that in a minute. First let's look at what we have in common. Reason is what led Descartes to say, 'I think, therefore I am.' It's the basic functioning of logic in our minds. Descartes realized that he couldn't even think if he didn't exist. Without reason, we couldn't know anything at all."

"No problem there."

"And experience is what we observe. It's close to the empiricism you used to believe in, but it doesn't pretend to stand all alone. Experience is what we see, hear, smell, taste, or feel."

"Right. And I think that's the most reliable way to know things."

"Some things. But it's pretty impractical for other things."

"Like what?"

"Like things that can't be observed empirically, for one thing. And for another thing, if our knowledge were limited to our own experience, none of us would know much. In fact, probably most of what we know doesn't come by experience."

"Oh?"

"Sure. Where's the White House?"

"In Washington."

"Ever seen it there?"

"No. I mean, yes. I've seen pictures of it on the news."

"But you haven't been there yourself and seen it?"

"No. Not yet anyway."

"So you trust someone who tells you about it—tells you what's in the picture, where the picture was taken, and so on?"

"Right."

"Well, then you take some of your knowledge from authority, not experience."

"Sure. I guess everybody does."

"And even your own experience you don't trust completely, right?"

"What do you mean?"

"Remember when we studied naive realism in epistemology last spring?"

"Sure. Sometimes our senses mislead us, and we have to correct them. Like when a straight stick extends under water and looks bent at the surface. The appearance is deceiving. But we can also make up for it because we know *why* it is deceiving: because water refracts light differently from air."

"Exactly. So while experience isn't absolutely trustworthy, we have learned to test and qualify it so we can trust a great deal of what we learn by it."

"But not everything."

"Right. And the third way of knowing things is authority."

"You mean, believe me because I say so? I'm not that gullible, Jim."

"No, I mean believing things on the basis of *credible* authority—authority that deserves our trust."

"Look, Jim. I get the sneaking suspicion you're about to ask me to swallow a bunch of things just because somebody says so."

"Never, Dave. But I do want you to agree that legitimate authority is one way we know things. For instance, you believe the earth moves around the sun. Have you ever done the astronomical experiments necessary to prove that?"

"Of course not."

"So you believe it because people you respect as truthful and capable astronomers tell you what the experiments show. And even if you did the experiments yourself, you'd be depending on the validity of geometric theorems you've never tested. You trust them because you're confident that the mathematicians who have tested them did their tests right and were honest about the results."

"All right."

"Think about it, Dave. Life would be impossible for us if we never trusted authority. Every moment we would face choices we couldn't resolve without first testing truths we now take for granted. Whatever we don't know through either pure reason or pure experience, we have to accept on authority or remain ignorant."

"True. But authority isn't always as reliable as pure reason."

"Not always. I'll grant that. But neither is experience. Pure reason affords absolute proof of some things—things susceptible of being known by reason alone. But those things don't tend to be very significant. They tend to be definitional or mathematical. Pure reason, for instance, tells us that all bachelors are unmarried men and that $2 + 2 = 4$. But it won't tell you whether it's safe to cross the street. And when it comes down to it, not much of your life depends on isolated definitions alone."

"I can see that. Like, I may not have absolute proof that I'll get across the street alive, but I still cross when I think it's safe."

"Right. And even though your senses aren't 100 percent reliable, still you take 100 percent of yourself across the street. You commit yourself completely to something for which you don't have 100 percent proof."

"How come I get the feeling again that you're about to ask me to commit myself to something without good reasons?"

"Your basic skepticism, I guess. And if somebody were to do that to me, I'd walk away. But that's not what I'm about to do. I just want to be sure you're willing to apply the same, everyday criteria to God that you do to everyday life-and-death decisions.

"Imagine, for instance, that you are standing in a sixth-floor room in a burning building. You're convinced that if you stay there you will burn to death. You're also pretty sure that if you jump, you'll break your leg or kill yourself, or at least knock yourself silly and die when the building collapses on top of you.

But you've got a chance that way. If you stay, you're dead. What will you do?"

"Jump, I guess."

"Despite the danger? Why?"

"Because I'd consider the slight chance of survival by jumping more attractive than the near certainty of death if I don't."

"Precisely. You would never jump if the building weren't burning, or if there weren't some better avenue of escape. So the stakes involved in a decision can justify our trusting some things on little evidence or with little certitude that we would not ordinarily trust on much greater evidence."

"What does this have to do with whether God exists?"

"We're dealing with a question that can't be answered by pure reason alone—math or logic. It must be answered by some combination of reason, experience, and authority. The evidence will differ from the certainty afforded by pure reason, but it will be evidence of something more significant than mere definitions, and the stakes involved are considerably higher. So a solid decision will still make sense."

"It still sounds like you're just making excuses in advance for weak arguments."

"Why?"

"Because you're setting me up to make a decision based on only slight evidence. I want good reasons for believing in God, not lousy ones."

"So do I, and I think I have them. But let me ask you something: If you'd been in the burning building, with no alternatives in sight, would you have demanded strong evidence that you'd survive before you jumped?"

"If there were no other alternatives?"

"Right."

"Well, I would have chosen whichever alternative offered the better chance of survival."

"Even if the chance it offered were small?"

"If it were better than the alternative, yes."

"All right. If that kind of decision-making is acceptable in the case of preserving your physical life, why shouldn't it be acceptable in the case of committing yourself—or not committing yourself—to God?"

"For one thing, I think there would be more options in the case of God."

"Oh? What are they?"

"Well, I could withhold judgment, for one thing."

"You mean be neutral? But don't you see that that's not a third option at all?"

"What do you mean?"

"The two options are committing yourself or not committing yourself. Withholding judgment means not committing yourself."

"Oh, I see. But it isn't a permanent decision. I can change my mind later."

"Yes, perhaps you can. And perhaps you can change your mind later if you commit yourself, too. But at any given time, you've made a decision either for or against God. I'm going to argue that just as in the case of the burning building there comes a time when that decision can't be put off, so in the case of your committing yourself or not committing yourself to God there comes a time when that decision can't be put off. If that time should come, would you commit yourself based even on a merely slight preponderance of evidence, or would you demand more?"

"I guess I see your point. If I were convinced that there were only the two options, and if the time came when I was convinced I had to make the decision, I'd make it even on only a slight preponderance of evidence."

"And might your decision be affected partly by the stakes involved?"

"What do you mean?"

"If it would be more advantageous to commit to God, even on only a slight preponderance of evidence, would you let that possible benefit affect your decision?"

"I don't know. That seems kind of self-centered."

"Is it any more self-centered than saving yourself from a burning building?"

"I suppose not."

"After all, how self-centered is it to save your life when doing so isn't going to hurt anybody else? If you're dead, you can't do anything for anybody else anyway."

"True."

"Then would you do it?"

"What—commit myself to God?"

"No. Would you let that benefit affect your decision?"

"I suppose so. But you still haven't shown me why I should believe God exists."

"Well, I've made a start anyway, with what we've said about the universe having been created. I'll be glad to give you more reasons."

"Another time, Jim. I'm getting sunburned—and so are you. Anyway, Sarah's expecting me to pick her up for dinner in an hour, and I've got to shower and dress first."

"Okay. Have a great evening, and say hello to her for me, will you?"

"Sure, Jim. And you do the same when you see Becky tonight. See you later."

Chapter 3

Again, Does God Exist?

Two weeks went by before Dave and Jim talked much about God again. Jim was frustrated. Every time he tried to broach the topic, Dave had some reason to go elsewhere. Except once, when Dave said he really wanted to talk—and then Jim had an appointment he couldn't break. Jim felt like their conversations were going nowhere. Their friendship seemed to have grown superficial.

But at last one day an opportunity came again. Jim and his friend Doug—a young Christian Jim was helping with Bible study—were in Jim's apartment when Dave came by. To Jim's surprise, Dave brought the subject up again himself.

"Jim, remember a while ago we were talking about God and stuff? You said you could give me more reasons to believe in Him. Well, I've been thinking about it, and I'd like to hear your reasons."

"Great. I thought you'd never ask."

"You sound like you're a hound dog fresh on the scent! Trying to convert me or something?"

"Of course!"

"Come on, Jim, don't give me that. One of the things I've liked about you is that you're willing to just talk things through, not browbeat me. You don't seem like you're trying to convert me."

"Well, I am, but I'm not. I know I can't do anything to *make* you believe. All the arguments in the world won't force that. But I do hope to remove some of the obstacles in your way. And then, of course, if you do believe, I'll be delighted."

"Okay, I can live with that. So tell me, why should I believe in God?"

"First, because reason and experience have led us to believe that the universe was created. Christianity calls the Creator God. Second, because reason and experience have led us to believe that the universe must have been created by some intelligent and all-powerful being. Again, Christianity calls that being God. Third, because God Himself has told us He exists. That's revelation, that special kind of authority I told you about before. And fourth, because God became a man in Jesus Christ and showed Himself to us."

"Hold on, Jim. I don't buy all that!"

"You've already agreed to the first two points."

"Sure, but not the last two. Those are crazy. You can't prove those."

"Well, we'll get to those. But for now let's focus on the first two for a minute. You agree that the universe has a Creator/Designer?"

"Yes, I guess so."

"And that the Creator/Designer is intelligent and powerful?"

"I suppose so."

"All he's telling you by the first two points," Doug interrupted, "is that Christianity calls this Creator/Designer God. After all, you've got to call Him something, and throughout history philosophers and religious people have called Him God."

"I suppose they have. But listen—why should the Creator not have been created itself? I mean, if there is a Creator, where did it come from?"

"Nowhere," said Doug. "He always existed."

"Then why not say the universe always existed and dispense with the need for the Creator?"

"Because entropy shows that the material universe can't be eternal," Jim reminded him. "It's headed for maximum randomness, and since it isn't there now, it can't have been headed that way forever. So it has to have come into existence. Remember?"

"Yes, but you haven't really solved the problem any more by bringing God into the picture than I have. Why shouldn't the Creator have been created by something else?"

"Because in any chain of cause and effect, either there is a first cause or there isn't. The chain of cause and effect can't be circular, because then each effect would be both before and after itself. And the chain can't be infinite either, because then there would be no explanation for anything."

"I'm not sure I follow that," Doug said.

"It's called the principle of contingency. Effects don't explain themselves. If everything were contingent—if everything were an effect—then nothing would be explained at all. But there must be a reason for the existence of the universe, since once it didn't exist and later it did. If there is a reason for anything to exist, then there must be something that isn't contingent, something uncaused—eternal."

"Fair enough," said Dave. "But that doesn't tell us the Creator of the universe has existed forever. It only tells us that *something* has."

"Precisely. Nothing I've said so far tells us the *universe's* cause is the *First* Cause. But Christians believe God tells us so by revelation.

"Look, reason tells us you can have neither an infinite nor a circular chain of cause and effect. So if there is a chain—and we agree there is, since the universe itself is an effect—then there must be a First Cause somewhere along the line. All I'm telling you is that Christians believe the Creator/Designer of the universe is the First Cause, and that the First Cause is God, and that we believe that because God Himself tells us so. Of course, we also believe a lot more about God than that He's the First Cause, but we do believe that."

"All right. But what about your two other reasons for believing God exists?"

"First a point of clarification. At this point, we're not really talking about whether God—if we define God as the First Cause, the intelligent and powerful Creator/Designer of the universe—whether God exists. We're really talking about what God is like. Fair enough?"

"What do you mean?"

"Well, we've already agreed that there is an uncaused Cause of the universe, a Creator/Designer. For the sake of our discussion, can we agree to call Him God?"

"I guess there's no reason not to."

"All right, then," said Jim. "We know what God is like because He has told us about Himself by revelation and because He became a man in Jesus Christ to show us Himself. So if we really want to know what God is like, the best way is to meet Jesus. The Bible tells us about Him."

Dave wasn't sure he liked the direction the conversation was taking. Besides, something else was eating away at his mind. Something he'd thought little about before because it hadn't seemed important. After all, since he'd been an atheist, it hadn't seemed to matter. But if he were on the verge of believing in God, he had to think it through more carefully.

"Look, guys, there's something else that's bugging me, and I don't think I can go much farther in this conversation without addressing it."

"What's that, Dave?"

"Well, you believe God is good, right?"

"Of course," said Doug.

"And you believe He's so intelligent that all the information in the universe doesn't equal His intelligence, right?"

"True."

"And you believe He's powerful, right?"

"Yes."

"More powerful than all the power in the universe?"

"Right."

"Then how come there's evil?"

"Good question," Jim said.

"I mean, an all-powerful, all-knowing, all-good God wouldn't permit evil to exist. But evil *does* exist. So either God doesn't exist at all, or He's pretty different from what you believe He is."

Jim paused for a moment. He'd expected this argument to come up sometime. He hoped he was ready for it. He had answers he found satisfactory. Getting them across to someone like Dave was another question. But Doug spoke up first.

"Dave, that's one of the toughest arguments against God. But I think there are good answers to it."

"I'm listening."

"If I understand correctly," Doug said, "you're saying that it is logically inconsistent both to believe that an all-powerful, all-knowing, all-good God exists and to believe that evil exists. Right?"

"Exactly."

"So to answer your argument, I need to show that there is some way in which the two beliefs can be consistent, right?"

"Right."

"And if there were some third proposition that was consistent with both, that would prove the consistency of the two?"

"Run that by me again."

"No matter how much A and B *appear* to be incompatible, if I can show that C is compatible with both, then A and B are not incompatible."

"Okay, that makes sense."

"Well, I'd like to suggest as a third proposition the following: 'It would be morally better for God to create a world containing free beings than for Him to create a world without them.'"

Jim thought of interrupting. He anticipated trouble down the road if Doug used this argument. But he thought he'd sit back and see first where it led. He figured Dave would probably see a hole in it.

"I don't see how that ties the first two together at all," Dave said.

"I admit it's not immediately apparent. It might be easier to come at it from a different direction. Have you ever done anything really mean to anybody—your sister or somebody?"

"Well, sure. I threw a can of salmon in her hair the night of the senior prom, for one thing."

"Boy, I bet she was mad!"

"She sure was."

"Is she still mad at you?"

"No. In fact, after I did it, I realized how rotten it was, and I was really sorry. So I told her so, and she actually forgave me."

"Perfect! That's just what I was looking for."

"What do you mean?"

"Think about it for a minute," said Doug. "Do you admire your sister for forgiving you? Are you glad she did? Do you think it was something exceptional, something really good for her to do?"

"Yes, I do. But I don't see what this has to do with God and evil."

"Just this—could your sister ever have forgiven you if you had never done anything wrong to her?"

"No."

"And isn't forgiveness one of the highest goods we know? The old moral philosophers called it a high virtue. You'd agree, wouldn't you?"

"Yes, I guess so."

"And aren't there other high virtues that could never occur if there weren't evil?"

"Yes, I see. There couldn't be courage without danger and fear, or mercy without ill desert—"

"Or compassion without suffering, or patience without trials—"

"Or even the vindication of someone who'd been wronged without his having been wronged in the first place," said Dave.

"Right!" Doug said. "Even punishment of a crime is a truly good thing, but it couldn't happen without there being a crime to punish. In fact, all the highest virtues come into play in response to evils."

"So you're saying God allows evil as a way of achieving some higher good?"

"Yes."

"But isn't that the same as saying the end justifies the means? I heard Jim argue against that in ethics class, when we were studying utilitarianism."

"True. Do you remember his argument?"

"If I recall, Jim, you reminded us of Jean-Paul Sartre's story *The Wall*, in which some jailed revolutionary decided to play games with the police by lying to them about the rebel leader's hiding-place. The next thing he knew, the police were dragging the leader in. He'd been right where the other guy said he was—even though he'd thought he'd been lying."

"And what principle did Jim draw from that?" Doug asked.

"Well, the guy couldn't *know* that his lie would achieve a good end, so he couldn't justify the evil means by appealing to the intended good end."

"Right. And what was the crucial problem with his reasoning?"

"His limited knowledge."

"Exactly. So would that argument apply against God's justifying the means by the end?"

"I see what you mean," said Dave. "If God is all-knowing, He can really know the ends that any means will achieve."

"Precisely," said Doug. "Now, let's get back to the logical question of God and evil. You were arguing that if God were all-good, all-powerful, and all-knowing, there shouldn't be any evil. I suggested that it would be better for God to create a universe containing free moral beings than a universe without them, and that that would show the consistency of believing in God and recognizing the evil in the universe."

"Right. It's still not clear to me how that solves your problem."

"The key question is, 'What is a morally free being?'"

"Somebody who can choose between good and evil, I suppose," said Dave.

"Yes. And that implies that he can choose evil instead of good."

"Right. But why would it be better to create things that could choose evil? Why not only things that could choose good?"

"Because their freedom to choose endows them with responsibility and dignity and accountability," Doug said. "Look at it this way. If you do something wrong, people can blame you for it. But if you do something right, they can praise you for it. It's your freedom that makes the praise or the blame sensible. After all, nobody praises a hammer for driving in nails or blames it for clubbing somebody over the head, right?"

"Right."

"Why not?"

"Because the hammer doesn't make the choice. It isn't free."

"Exactly. But you are. Now, which would you prefer—to be yourself, capable of right and wrong and so susceptible of praise or blame, or to be the hammer, capable of neither right nor wrong and so susceptible of neither praise nor blame?"

"Myself, obviously."

"Good. Now, if God is morally good, and if it is better to create a world with morally free beings than without them, then if God creates anything, He should create a world with morally free beings. But such a world is one in which evil is possible. That means our first proposition (God exists and is all-powerful, all-knowing, and all-good) is compatible with a third (It is better to create a world with morally free beings than without them) that entails at least the possibility of the second (There is evil in the world). This means God's existence and the reality of evil are not logically contradictory to each other. They are compatible."

Now Jim intervened. It was clear to him what this argument implied about God, even if it wasn't clear to Doug. "There's just one problem, Doug."

"What's that?"

"Do you praise God for His goodness?"

"Of course I do."

"Why?"

"Because He deserves that praise, that's why."

Dave caught on. "Then do you believe God could choose evil?" he asked.

51

"Of course not! God's perfect; He couldn't choose evil."

"Then what was all that baloney you gave me about morally free beings deserving praise when they choose good and blame when they choose evil, but non-free beings not deserving praise or blame?"

"I—I never thought of it that way."

Doug was flustered, and Dave wasn't about to let him off the hook.

"Look, Doug," Dave said, "you've argued that something only deserves praise for doing good if it had the choice of doing evil instead. But now you're telling me God couldn't choose evil. That means God doesn't deserve praise for doing good. But if He deserves praise for doing good, then He could choose evil. So either God isn't really all good—which means you've conceded my point anyway—or He isn't morally free and so shouldn't be praised for doing good."

"Dave's right, Doug," Jim said. "That's why I don't use that kind of argument to answer the problem of evil. I know a lot of Christians do. In fact, I used to. But ultimately I think the argument fails, and Dave hit its weak point right on the head."

"All right, Jim, then how *do* you answer?" asked Doug.

"Well, your answer wasn't entirely wide of the mark, Doug. Your problem was in rooting it in a definition of moral freedom that entailed the possibility of choosing evil. That isn't what the Bible means by moral freedom. In Romans 6, the Bible says that before conversion, everyone is enslaved to sin—evil. But when people are converted, when they become Christians, God sets them free from their slavery to sin. The Bible defines moral freedom not as the capacity to choose either good or evil but as the capacity to choose, with unmixed motives, what is really good. More precisely, the Bible defines moral freedom as the freedom to act consistently with one's own moral nature, if that nature is good. So God is morally free in that nothing can make Him do anything against His nature, and His nature is perfectly good. In fact, it is the perfection of His moral nature that makes Him most worthy of praise. And it also means that He can't choose evil."

Dave had a response to that. "But, Jim, I don't buy everything in the Bible. Why should I buy that answer?"

"At this point I'm not asking you to buy it, Dave. I'm just asking you to understand what kind of God, and what kind of ethics, real Christianity is talking about. Whether you buy it is another matter."

Now Doug had questions of his own. "But if moral freedom doesn't entail the capacity to choose evil, then how can you reconcile God and evil?"

"Reconcile God and evil? I don't!" said Jim. "I don't reconcile God and evil because God hates evil. God can never be reconciled with evil."

"But then why does He allow it to exist?" Dave asked.

"Because—and here's where Doug's answer was right— He has purposes for it, purposes that are truly good."

"Like?"

"Well, those virtues you talked about, for starters. Mercy and forgiveness and compassion and courage and vindication of the oppressed are really good things, and none of them would come into action if there were no evil. But you were focusing on those qualities in people. That's important, but it isn't the ultimate reason for the existence of evil. The ultimate reason is to display to all creation those qualities in God Himself."

Now Doug was puzzled. "Where do you get that idea, Jim? I've never heard that before."

"From the Bible, of course. Where I go for everything I know about God. For instance, the Apostle Paul explains in Ephesians 1:6 that the ultimate goal God has in mind in freeing some people from evil is 'the praise of the glory of His grace.' He gets more explicit in Ephesians 2:7, in which he writes that God's intention in saving some people is 'that in the ages to come He might show the exceeding riches of His grace in His kindness toward us in Christ Jesus.' In Romans 9:22-23, Paul explains that God demonstrates both His justice in punishing evil and His grace in pardoning people, and that these both show His glory."

"But that sounds like pride and selfishness to me," Doug said.

"Me, too," Dave added.

"But the problem is in us, not in God," Jim countered.

"How come?" Doug asked.

"Because if God really is the all-good, all-powerful, all-knowing Creator of the universe, and if His justice really is a good thing and does good in punishing evil, and if His grace really is a good thing and does good in pardoning evil, then He thoroughly deserves the glory and praise He expects from His creatures, and it isn't at all selfish or prideful for Him both to require it and to order the universe so as to elicit it."

"Boy, that's a new way of looking at things for me," Doug said.

"Exactly. It's a completely different way of looking at things from how you began your answer to Dave's question. Your answer assumed that the universe existed for man's benefit—to instill virtues in man. Now, it's great to instill virtues in man, but the Bible says that isn't the highest purpose of creation. It's to display the glory, the goodness, the justice, the grace—all the perfections—of God, its Creator, Judge, and Savior. That's why Revelation 4:11 says that in heaven people worship God, saying, 'You are worthy, O Lord, to receive glory and honor and power; for You have created all things, and by Your will they exist and were created!'"[3]

"I think I see it," Dave said. "Your answer to evil is God-centered. Doug's was man-centered."

"Right," Jim said.

"Boy," Doug said. "I'd never noticed that before. Here I've been belly-aching against the influence of humanism in our society ever since I became a Christian, and yet I've been thinking humanistically."

"Why do you say that?" Dave asked.

"Because my argument made man the measure—the standard—of all things, and that's the essence of humanism. Jim's argument makes God the standard."

"I see. But I'm not at all sure I accept Jim's argument, or its conclusions."

"I don't expect you to accept it right away, Dave. I'm simply telling you what Christianity says is the answer to your problem. It comes as part of the package of Christianity. You see, you really can't choose to believe a little bit of the Christian faith and not all of it. All truth is unified, and you either buy the whole package or you reject it. If you latch onto some but reject other parts, you're really just being inconsistent."

"All right, let me see if I'm following you. You say that God permits evil—"

"More than that—that God planned the occurrence of evil in His universe from the beginning."

"Okay, that God planned evil in order to display His own perfection?"

"Right."

"Well, I'm not sure I can agree, but go ahead."

"All right. The Bible says the highest way in which evil serves the purpose of displaying God's perfection was in God's simultaneously punishing evil and, by taking the punishment on Himself, pardoning those who have done it."

"How did He do that?"

"Let me ask you a question first. Think about some of the war movies you've seen. In a good many, what is the noblest act you see?"

"When somebody gives his life up to save his buddies."

"Right. Like John Paul in an old John Wayne movie. Kirk Douglas plays a pilot who's generally a scoundrel, but one day he purposely flies a reconnaissance plane right out in the open above an enemy fleet, knowing he'll get shot down, so he can give an accurate intelligence report to the base and enable the American forces to prepare for battle."

"Yeah, I saw that one. He gets shot down, and everybody considers him a hero despite his mean streak."

"Okay, so self-sacrifice on his part demonstrated some nobility. It even served to counterbalance, at least a little bit, his vicious streak."

"Right."

"Well, in that case, John Paul sacrificed himself for his friends. Suppose instead someone showed such great love that he sacrificed himself for his enemies—that he took on himself the death they deserved."

"That would be even more admirable, I guess," Dave said.

"The greatest such self-sacrifice, according to Christianity, was when God became a man in Jesus Christ, took the punishment on sin demanded by His own justice, and thereby paid the penalty so that all who believe in Him could be pardoned for their sin."

"That doesn't make much sense to me," Dave said. "Why was such a sacrifice necessary?"

"Because people need to be spared two kinds of evil: sin and suffering. Christianity says all men are sinners—we all do evil. We're enslaved to it, according to Romans 6, until God sets us free in Christ. It is an evil that we are enslaved to sin. But our sin also has evil consequences. Directly, it causes us and others to suffer. And indirectly, it draws on us more suffering because God's justice requires that we be punished for it. So the problem of evil for God—if we can call it that—was how God could both satisfy the demands of His justice to punish sin and yet deliver people from suffering punishment for sin. His solution was to bear the punishment Himself, satisfying the demands of justice, and to forgive sinners, crediting His own perfection to them. All this, Christianity says, God achieved by Christ's death on the cross when He suffered the penalty for our sins in our place."

"But look, Jim, I'll concede that everybody does things wrong every once in a while. But we're not completely evil. Why should we deserve such punishment that only God could bear it for us?"

"The question is whether we sin at all. Do you do everything you know you ought, and nothing you know you ought not? Have you never done anything wrong in all your life— never lied, cheated, stolen, coveted what belonged to someone else? Hated someone?"

"Well, yes, I've done those things, but I'm not really that bad."

"By whose standard, Dave?"

"Well, compared with a lot of people—"

"Like Hitler and Stalin and Mao Tse-tung and Pol Pot and Charles Manson?"

"Sure, those guys, but even people I know. Lots of ordinary people are a lot worse than I am."

"I don't doubt it, Dave. In fact, I think of you as a pretty good guy. But you know what mistake we're making?"

"No, what?"

"Same mistake I made earlier," Doug said. "Humanism."

"What?"

"Making man the standard."

"Oh, I see," said Dave. "I'm measuring myself compared with other people, not with God."

"Right," Jim said. "And God's standard is Himself. Do you measure up to that standard?"

"Well, not exactly."

"Neither does anybody else, Dave. But this is why Jesus Christ is so important. He's God's answer to the problem of evil. God is dealing with evil by saving men from its power over them, by using it to make them better—building virtues they couldn't have without it—and by showing His justice in punishing it and His grace in pardoning it. And He's doing all this through Jesus' death as our substitute, bearing the punishment for sin, and His resurrection from the dead, conquering evil. This is how, as Paul put it in Romans 3:26, God was able to 'be just and the justifier of the one who has faith in Jesus.'"

"Look, Jim, I don't know what to say right now. This is all new to me. Give me a few days to think it over. Then I want to talk again."

"Sure, Dave. I can't blame you. I'm asking you to take on a whole new way of understanding all of reality. It makes sense that it should take some time and careful thought."

Chapter 4

What Are the Evidences for Christianity?

It was just a day later when Dave and Jim got together again, again in Jim's apartment. This time Dave was ready to talk immediately. He had some new questions on his mind.

"Listen, Jim, I think we're getting ahead of ourselves. You're trying to persuade me to embrace the whole of Christian faith. I'm not prepared for that. After all, just a month ago I was an atheist. I can see now what's wrong with atheism. But plenty of philosophers have been agnostics, and others are humanists. They don't see any need to profess the Christian faith. I think I'm more likely to find myself in one of those camps."

"Humanism perhaps, Dave, but not agnosticism. That's not for you. You've already concluded that God exists, right?"

"Maybe, but maybe not. It depends on how you define God. I really don't think we know much about God."

"Well, Dave, there are two kinds of agnostics: those who

simply say *they* don't know if God exists, and those who say *no one* can know. The second kind is really saying he knows the minds of all people and knows what is and isn't possible for them to know. That's pretty presumptuous, isn't it?"

"Yes. I'm not saying that at all."

"So you're just saying that *you* don't know if God exists—or, to put it more accurately, what God's like?"

"Right."

"So you're not denying that other people might know?"

"Right."

"Then you should be open, since you say you yourself don't know, to learning from those who say they do know."

"Sounds reasonable. But that doesn't mean I have to buy into everything the first guy I meet tells me."

"Of course not. Just that you should be willing to consider carefully what someone says."

"Yes. But there's also humanism. I think I find that philosophy pretty attractive."

"What do you mean by humanism, Dave?"

"Well, according to the *Humanist Manifestoes I & II*, whether there is a God or not, mankind should look to himself for solutions to his problems. We shouldn't try to escape our problems by shifting them off on a God we really don't know anything about."

"That's one kind of humanism, Dave, and it's obviously anti-Christian. Originally, though, humanism was the belief that man and his works—literature, art, science, music, drama, etc.—were legitimate objects of study. That may seem obvious to us today, but there was a period in the Western world, at least, when most people thought the only proper objects of study were God and His works—religion, essentially. Originally humanism simply reminded us that it was okay to study things outside religion; but it wasn't anti-religious.

"Christianity welcomed the original kind of humanism.

In fact, some of the greatest early humanists were Christians—people like Erasmus and Martin Luther and John Calvin—all of whom lived at the time of the Reformation, in the sixteenth century. Despite their doctrinal differences, they all professed Christian faith and would have been called humanists by the original definition. But Christianity rejects modern humanism because it leaves the most important Being in all existence out of the picture and falsely exalts man, claiming he is better than he really is."

"So you're saying we really do need God to solve our problems. That doesn't mean God actually exists, you know. Aren't you just wishing this stuff were true because it would be comforting to you if it were?"

"No, no! I don't believe in God—or in the whole of Christian teaching—because I wish it were true. I believe for lots of good reasons. Of course you're right—wishing doesn't make something true. But wishing doesn't make something false either."

"All right. We've talked about some of your reasons for believing in God. What about the rest of your Christian faith? You've been talking about Jesus Christ. But in a course on ancient myths that I took a couple of years ago, the professor said there really wasn't even very good evidence that Jesus ever lived—let alone that he was the Son of God or anything else that Christianity teaches about Him."

Jim almost heaved an audible sigh of relief. He'd wondered when their conversations would ever reach this point. He'd prayed for this moment time and again. Now it was here. He didn't want to waste it.

"It's really pretty irresponsible historically for the professor to have said that," he said.

"Why?"

"Because there's more and better historical evidence that

Jesus existed, and for the various things Christians believe He did, than there is for just about anyone else in antiquity."

"Oh? Evidence like what?"

"The New Testament, for one thing."

"You mean the Bible? But that's a Christian book."

"Well, it's part of the Bible. Actually it's twenty-seven different writings, the first four of which are entirely devoted to telling about the ministry, death, and resurrection of Jesus, and the fifth of which tells the history of the earliest Christians. These documents give quite strong evidence about Jesus, His claims, and His deeds."

"But they were all written by His followers, weren't they?"

"True—although many of the books of the New Testament were written by a man who at first approved of Jesus' murder and then persecuted His followers, even to the point of having some of them killed. But there are other evidences for Jesus, too. For instance, the Jewish historian Flavius Josephus, not a Christian, wrote about Jesus in his *Antiquities of the Jews*."

Jim reached over to his bookshelf and picked up a copy of David Noebel's *Understanding the Times*, remembering that it quoted Josephus. "Let me read to you what Josephus wrote," he said, "so you don't have to rely on my memory alone. In describing the period of Pontius Pilate, the Roman governor of Judea, Josephus wrote,

> "'At this time there was a wise man who was called Jesus. And his conduct was good, and [he] was known to be virtuous. And many people from among the Jews and other nations became his disciples. Pilate condemned him to be crucified and to die. And those who had become his disciples did not abandon his discipleship. They reported that he had appeared to them three days after his crucifixion

and that he was alive; accordingly, he was perhaps the messiah concerning whom the prophets have recounted wonders.'"[4]

"When did this Josephus write his history, though? Was it a long time later?"

"No; he wrote late in the first century, completing it around A.D. 93 or 94. He is one of the primary sources of information about late Jewish history. Roman historians confirm Jesus' existence, too. Look here: Cornelius Tacitus, writing around A.D. 112 about the reign of Nero, wrote of 'the persons commonly called Christians' and said, 'Christus, the founder of the name, was put to death by Pontius Pilate, procurator of Judea in the reign of Tiberius: but the pernicious superstition, repressed for a time broke out again, not only through Judea, where the mischief originated, but through the city of Rome also.'[5] Suetonius mentioned Jesus in his *Life of Claudius*, written around A.D. 120, and Pliny the Younger wrote of Jesus in a letter around A.D. 112."[6]

"But these hardly substantiate all the claims Christians make about Jesus. I'll grant that somebody named Jesus lived back then, but everything you believe about Him? Not hardly."

"Patience, patience. We're just getting started. A medical doctor named Luke became an associate of some of the early Christians. He wrote two of the first five books of the New Testament—the Gospel of Luke and the Acts of the Apostles. His care as a historian was demonstrated by painstaking research by a British historian and archaeologist, Sir William Ramsay, who confirmed Luke's accuracy even in minute details through archaeological research. In the introduction to his Gospel, Luke assured the friend to whom he was writing that he intended to convey the most carefully researched historical facts."

Jim opened his Bible to Luke 1 and began reading:

> "'Inasmuch as many have taken in hand to set in order a narrative of those things which which are most surely believed among us, just as those who from the beginning were eyewitnesses and ministers of the word delivered them to us, it seemed good to me also, having had perfect understanding of all things from the very first, to write to you an orderly account, most excellent Theophilus, that you may know the certainty of those things in which you have been instructed.'"

Dave was listening intently. He'd never heard before that Christianity stood on historical evidence. Jim was determined to make the best of the opportunity.

"When Luke began writing about the public works of Jesus," Jim said, turning to Luke 3, "he put it in a historical setting:

> "'Now in the fifteenth year of the reign of Tiberius Caesar, Pontius Pilate being governor of Judea, Herod being tetrarch of Galilee, his brother Philip tetrarch of Iturea and the region of Trachonitis, and Lysanias tetrarch of Abilene, Annas and Caiaphas being high priest. . . .'

"That has the ring of real history to it, doesn't it?"

"I'm not sure what you mean," Dave said.

"Well, compare that language with the language of myths and fairy tales you've heard. They don't begin by precisely pinpointing the time when something happened. Instead, they start out with 'Once upon a time' or something like that."

"True."

"Well, the other three Gospels—Matthew, Mark, and John—also contain clear historical references. They were written by people who respected historical fact. Two of these men, Matthew and John, were followers of Jesus during His ministry. One, Mark, was the close friend of another follower, Peter (who himself wrote two short letters in the New Testament). Luke was a close companion first of Peter and then of Paul and several others of Jesus' followers and recorded not only the life and teachings of Jesus but also the lives and works of His closest followers and their first followers in the Book of Acts."

"That's not the impression I got when I took that course on mythology," Dave said.

"I'm not surprised. Lots of people downplay the historical underpinnings of Christianity—sometimes through ignorance, but sometimes because they oppose it."

"You know, it was pretty obvious that Professor Millard was pretty hostile to Christianity. He got a real charge out of confusing the few Christians who dared to speak up in his classes."

"I know," said Jim. "I was one of them a couple of years ago. It was partly his challenges that motivated me to learn this stuff. And since then, I've found that we actually know more about the life, teachings, birth, and death of Jesus than about almost any other figure in the ancient world."

"Okay, Jim, I suppose there's no doubt Jesus existed. But why should I believe He's God in the flesh? Can't I just think of Him as a good moral teacher?"

"Well, you could, but it would be pretty silly. Do good moral teachers knowingly teach things they know are false?"

"No, I suppose not."

"And they don't make grandiose claims about themselves—particularly if the claims are false?"

"Certainly not."

"And they don't claim to be God, do they?"

"No. But did Jesus really claim that?"

"Yes. Let me give you a few examples."

"Fire away."

Turning to John 14:9-11, Jim said, "First, one of the ways Jews referred to God in Jesus' day was as 'the Father.' Once one of Jesus' followers, Philip, asked Him to show them God the Father. Jesus responded, 'Have I been with you so long, and yet you have not known Me, Philip? He who has seen Me has seen the Father; so how can you say, "Show us the Father"? Do you not believe that I am in the Father, and the Father in Me? . . . Believe Me that I am in the Father and the Father in Me, or else believe Me for the sake of the works themselves.'"

Flipping back to John 10, Jim continued, "Another time Jesus was assuring His followers that the Father would take care of them after He had left them. He concluded by saying, 'I and the Father are one.' The Jewish leaders who opposed Him understood this as a claim to be God, so they prepared to stone Him for blasphemy. What did Jesus do? Did He say, 'Hey, fellows, you've got it all wrong. You misunderstood Me. I didn't mean to say that I'm God'? Not at all. Instead, He said, 'Many good works I have shown you from My Father. For which of those works do you stone Me?' The Jews responded, 'For a good work we do not stone You, but for blasphemy, and because You, being a man, make Yourself God.' Again Jesus had the chance to clear up their misunderstanding—if they had misunderstood Him. But what He actually said just drove home His claim: 'If I do not do the works of My Father, do not believe Me; but if I do, though you do not believe Me, believe the works, that you may know and believe that the Father is in Me, and I in Him.'"

"I don't see how that means that Jesus was claiming to be God," Dave said.

"Well, maybe that's because you aren't a Jew living in Jesus' day. *They* understood it, and here's why: Nobody had ever claimed to be the Son of God among the Jews, and that's because they all realized that if God had a Son, that Son would have the same nature as God. Just as the son of a human being would be a human being, so the Son of God would be God."

"That makes sense, I guess."

"But that's not all we have to go on. In the Old Testament, the most common name for God is Yahweh, or Jehovah. Literally, it simply means 'I am.' The name expresses God's eternal existence, or, in terms borrowed from our earlier discussion, His non-contingency. Jesus claimed this name for Himself when He said, in John 8:24, '. . . if you do not believe that *I am* He, you will die in your sins.'"

"But couldn't He have been saying something less than that—perhaps that He was the Messiah they believed would come, or something like that?" Dave asked.

"In that instance, you might think so. But another time He made it crystal clear what He meant. He said later—also recorded in John 8, "Your father Abraham rejoiced to see My day, and he saw it and was glad. . . . Most assuredly, I say to you, before Abraham was, I AM.' There's no doubt what He meant there: He existed before Abraham, and He claimed the name of God as His own."

"I see. I never would have recognized that if I'd just read it myself, though."

"Well, you might have if you'd studied the Old Testament first, and thoroughly, as the Jews of Jesus' day had. At any rate, there's no doubt that *they* understood Him. But they didn't believe Him, so again they tried to stone Him for blasphemy."

Dave didn't respond for a long while. He was thinking, thinking hard. At last Jim said, "Dave, *some* of the Jews didn't believe Him. But others did. They became His followers—His disciples. The Apostle John, one of Jesus' closest friends—and who would be more likely to have seen His faults, if He'd had any?—called Him God in the opening verses of His Gospel. Thomas, after he'd seen Jesus risen from the dead, called Him his Lord and God (John 20:28). Peter, another of His closest friends, called Jesus God in the first verse of his second letter. The Apostle Paul—who opposed Jesus at first, remember—called Jesus God in his letter to Titus (2:13) and when speaking to Christian leaders in the city of Ephesus (Acts 20:28)."

"But that doesn't make it true," Dave said. "Just because somebody claims to be God—and some people even believe him—doesn't mean He really is."

"Right. But what are the alternatives in Jesus' case? We know He claimed to be God. If He isn't God, then how else might we explain that claim?"

Dave thought about it for a while. He didn't like the options. "Well," he finally said, "if He wasn't telling the truth, then He must either have been a horrible fraud or insane."

"I can't think of any other options," Jim said.

"But those don't sound very plausible," Dave added.

"Why not?" Jim asked.

"Well, because they don't fit Jesus' character, I guess. I mean, everybody recognizes Jesus as a great moral teacher. Someone like that wouldn't perpetrate lies like that—certainly nothing so enormous as that."

"It isn't very consistent, is it, with His saying that He was the way, the *truth*, and the life (John 14:6) and that the devil was a liar and the father of lies (John 8:44)?"

"I guess not. And from what little I understand, there isn't much likelihood that he was insane either."

"Why?"

"Well, because— Look, I may not know much about Christianity, but last week I read Jesus' Sermon on the Mount, and frankly, I think I never saw anything more sane in my life. If more people would live by what he says there, there'd be a lot less mental illness in this world."

Jim was surprised. "You've been reading the Bible lately?"

"Yeah, a little bit. I thought I ought to get acquainted with it for myself a little, so I started with the beginning of the New Testament."

"Not a bad idea. I hope you'll keep it up. It's the best way to get to know Jesus."

"We'll see."

"At any rate, Dave, I'm not surprised you didn't like the options when it came to explaining why Jesus would claim to be God."

"Oh?"

"No, because one of the most learned men of our century, C. S. Lewis—a professor of medieval and renaissance literature at Oxford and Cambridge—faced the same dilemma himself. He wrote about it in his book *Mere Christianity*." Jim got up and found the book, a well-worn paperback, on a shelf along with lots of others by Lewis. "Listen to this," he said, turning to the passage, which he'd marked when he'd read it for the first time six years before.

"'I am trying here to prevent anyone saying the really foolish thing that people often say about Him: "I'm ready to accept Jesus as a great moral teacher, but I don't accept His claim to be God." That is the one thing we must not say. A man who was merely a man and said the sort of things Jesus said would not be a great moral teacher. He would either be a lunatic—on a level with the man who says he is a poached egg—or else he would be the Devil of Hell. You must make your choice. Either this man was, and is, the Son of God: or else a madman or something worse. You can shut Him up for a fool, you can spit on Him and kill Him as a demon; or you can fall at His feet and call Him Lord and God. But let us not come with any patronizing nonsense about His being a great human teacher. He has not left that open to us. He did not intend to.'"

Answers for Atheists

"Lewis, by the way, was an atheist and then an agnostic before he became a Christian, and he wrote in his autobiography, *Surprised by Joy*, that he was driven into the faith by the overwhelming weight of the evidence."

Dave was deep in thought again. Something was beginning to dawn on him. But he was still wary.

"Of course," Jim said, "in the long run it's your decision. The only good way for you to decide whether you think Jesus was a liar or a lunatic or God in human flesh is to get to know Him. Read thoroughly about Him in the four Gospels and you'll have a clear picture of Jesus' character. Then decide for yourself."

"I guess I'll have to do that," Dave said. "But listen . . . What if Jesus never really said those things? Maybe his friends just made them up later. Maybe the Gospels aren't really accurate histories."

"Possible. Not likely, but possible."

"Why not likely?"

"Tell me, do people give their lives for something they know is a lie?"

"What's that got to do with it?"

"I'll tell you in a minute. First, just think about it: Do people give their lives for something they know is a lie?"

"Well, people have given their lives up for a lot of different religions."

"Yes, but when they did it, did they know those religions were lies?"

"I see what you mean. No, I suppose not. People might die for a lie without knowing it, but I can't imagine them dying for something they knew was false."

"Precisely. And eleven out of twelve of Jesus' foremost followers died for their faith. Jewish and Roman authorities who opposed Jesus and Christianity threatened to kill them unless they'd renounce their claim that Jesus was God and that

70

He'd risen from the dead. All twelve of them refused. Eleven were killed for their faith, and the twelfth—John—died in exile because he refused to say he'd been lying about Jesus."

"So whatever happened, they certainly didn't make up the stories," Dave said.

"Right. They really believed them."

"And they claimed to be eyewitnesses of Jesus' life and teachings?"

"Yes, they did."

"I guess they weren't lying then."

"No. And that conclusion is consistent with two other important things. First, historians and archaeologists— Christians and non-Christians alike—who specialize in studying the region and times of the New Testament are coming to realize increasingly how accurate and reliable the New Testament is as a collection of historical documents. They are finding again and again that if the New Testament says something happened, it happened. Here—you can read about it for yourself in this book." Jim tossed a copy of F. F. Bruce's *The New Testament Documents: Are They Reliable?* into Dave's lap. "And when you're done with that, I have a few others you can read here on the same subject.[8]

"A second reason why you should believe Jesus is who He said He is is that He claimed He would confirm His claims by rising from the dead. That miracle, He said, would be the chief sign that He was really the Son of God. His resurrection is the greatest proof of His deity. In fact, it's the greatest proof of the whole Christian faith, since all of that follows if Jesus really is God."

"Look, Jim, I'm getting tired. I confess you've given me a lot to think about here, but I'm afraid it's almost too much to digest. Give me some more time. We'll talk again; I promise. Particularly because I have some real problems with the last thing you said."

"Oh?"

"Yeah. See, I don't believe miracles are possible. It's the scientist in me, I guess."

"Well, I'll be glad to talk that issue through with you."

"Sure. But not right now. Next time, maybe."

Dave left the apartment—with the book Jim had tossed him.

Chapter 5

Did Jesus Really Rise from the Dead?

The very next day Dave was at Jim's door again. Now he was more eager than ever to talk.

"You know that book you loaned me last night?" he said. "Well, I could hardly put it down today. It's tough going, but it's really interesting. I never knew there was so much historical evidence for the Bible."

"Glad you're enjoying it," Jim said. "But last night you wound up by saying you couldn't believe in Jesus' resurrection because you think it's unscientific to believe in miracles, right?"

"Right. They're contrary to the laws of nature."

"So?"

"Well, the laws of nature can't be broken."

"And miracles, if they happened, would break them?"

"That's what I've always understood."

"Let me suggest another way to think of the laws of nature, Dave. The laws of nature don't tell us everything that can possibly happen. They just tell us what can happen *naturally*—that is, by nature working on its own. They don't tell us anything at all about what happens if something outside of nature acts *on* nature."

"But there isn't anything outside of nature."

"Really? I thought we'd been through that already. You remember—entropy, creation of the universe, God, all that?"

"Oh, yeah. I guess I was just following old habits of thinking."

"If there is something outside of nature that can affect nature, then things could happen in nature that nature itself couldn't bring about—and they wouldn't be contrary to the laws of nature at all."

"You mean, if God did something *to* nature, the results would be different than if He didn't?"

"Precisely. And we know that God can affect nature because, as we've already agreed, God is more powerful than all the power in the universe. He had to be, to create it."

"So a miracle, then, isn't a violation of the laws of nature at all?"

"No."

"It's just the effect of a cause outside nature acting within nature?"

"Right. The laws of nature tell us that certain kinds of effects follow certain kinds of causes. Introduce new causes, and you'll get new effects."

"I see! Natural causes produce natural effects. Unnatural causes produce unnatural effects." Dave himself was getting excited now.

"Exactly. And what I'm saying is that God—an unnatural Cause—reached into nature and added another factor into the chain of cause and effect, bringing about an effect not contrary to the laws of nature but beyond what nature by itself could have done—the resurrection of Jesus from the dead."

"Okay, I'll grant it's possible. But how do you *know* it? Just because it's possible doesn't mean it happened."

"The same way we know that Jesus claimed to be God: historical evidence."

"I'm listening."

"It'll help to set a little background first. Many times during His ministry, Jesus predicted that He would be crucified and that, following His death, He would rise again from the dead. A little over a week before His death, for instance, He told the disciples, '. . . we are going up to Jerusalem, and the Son of Man will be betrayed to the chief priest and to the scribes; and they will condemn Him to death, and deliver Him to the Gentiles to mock and to scourge and to crucify. And the third day He will rise again' (Matthew 20:18-19).[9]

"One curious thing is that His disciples did not understand these predictions. After one extraordinary event, Jesus instructed His disciples not to tell what they had seen 'till the Son of Man had risen from the dead.' Mark says, 'they kept this word to themselves, questioning what the rising from the dead meant.'"

"So the disciples weren't expecting Jesus to rise from the dead?"

"Right, Dave. That's why, although they had trusted Him before His death, afterward they were completely discouraged. In fact, most of them just went back to their former occupations. It looked like Christianity was dead forever."

"So when they did come to believe He'd risen from the dead, it couldn't have been because they were making it up, could it?" Dave asked.

"Right. In fact, He had to give them persuasive evidence Himself." Jim opened to Luke 24. "Once, while two disciples were walking along a road after His death, a fellow traveler approached them and remarked about how discouraged they seemed. They were surprised he didn't know why. 'Are you the only stranger in Jerusalem, and have you not known the things which have happened here in these days?' They explained to him that Jesus had died. Then they said, 'But we *were hoping* that it was He who was going to redeem Israel.' Notice that?"

"Yes. They *were hoping*, but by then they'd given up that hope."

"Exactly. But then the stranger responded, 'O foolish ones, and slow of heart to believe all that the prophets have spoken! Ought not the Christ to have suffered these things and to enter into His glory?' And he then showed them that a variety of passages in the Old Testament had predicted just this. Shortly, when they sat down to eat together, it was as if their eyes had been blinded but suddenly were opened, and they recognized that the Stranger was Jesus Himself."

"What kept them from recognizing Him before that?"

"I don't know exactly. The Bible doesn't say anything more than that they had been *kept* from recognizing Him. Another miracle, I guess. My own belief is that God did that to make an opportunity for Jesus to show them that the Old Testament had predicted all that, so they'd learn to trust—and study—the Old Testament more than they already did."

"It's clear, anyway, that they hadn't been expecting to see Him after He died."

"Yes. And shortly after that, when these two rejoined the other disciples in Jerusalem, they heard that Jesus had appeared to another of them—Peter (Luke 24:34). And while they were all together, Jesus Himself 'stood in the midst of them, and said to them, "Peace to you." But they were terrified and frightened, and supposed they had seen a spirit.'"

"Good grief, it takes them a while to learn, doesn't it?"

"It's amazing to me, too, Dave. But then I guess that says a lot for 20/20 hindsight. We weren't there at the time. Anyway, Jesus then said to them, 'Why are you troubled? And why do doubts arise in your hearts? Behold My hands and My feet, that it is I Myself. Handle Me and see, for a spirit does not have flesh and bones as you see I have.' They checked Him out, they watched Him eat bread and fish——"

"I suppose that rules out an illusion or a hallucination, doesn't it?" Dave said.

"I don't see any way around it. One of the disciples—Thomas—was a lot like you, Dave. He was really skeptical. He certainly wasn't in any hurry to believe that Jesus had risen from the dead, even when his best friends insisted they'd seen Him alive again. 'Unless I see in His hands the print of the nails, put my finger into the print of the nails, and put my hand into His side'—where the soldiers who crucified Him thrust a spear to make sure He was dead—'I will not believe,' Thomas said. Well, eight days later, Jesus appeared to all of them together. He said to Thomas, 'Reach your finger here, and look at My hands; and reach your hand here, and put it into My side. Do not be unbelieving, but believing.' Thomas responded by saying to Jesus, 'My Lord and my God!' (John 20:25-28)."

"So these guys weren't superstitious, were they?" Dave said. "They were pretty much like people today, demanding good evidence for extraordinary claims."

"Yes, they were. In fact, you could even go so far as to say they had the same scientific mind-set you have, Dave. They were so sure dead people couldn't come alive again that they wouldn't believe it of Jesus until they had seen solid proof. That's why Luke, in the introduction of his Acts of the Apostles, wrote that Jesus had presented Himself to the disciples alive 'by many infallible proofs.' The disciples were no gullible lightweights."

"True. But they were, after all, Jesus' best friends. Couldn't they just have dreamed up the story?"

"And died for what they knew was a lie?"

"No, I guess not."

"And besides, the Jewish and Roman leaders had a lot at stake in keeping people believing Jesus was still dead. If the disciples had just made up the story, the leaders could have simply trotted out the body and squashed the whole charade. But when they went to the cave—the tomb—they found nothing."

"I hadn't thought of that."

"And then there's Saul of Tarsus."

"Oh? Who's he?"

"Saul was his Hebrew name. I've mentioned him before as Paul—his Roman name."

"Oh, yeah. The man who opposed Jesus and persecuted His followers."

"Right. His changed heart is one of the strongest reasons to believe the disciples never made up the story."

"How's that?"

"Well, he said that seeing the risen, living Jesus after His death was what changed him from an enemy to a friend—from a skeptic to a believer who went all over the world telling people about Jesus and finally gave his life for his preaching. Acts 9 records his conversion. No made-up story by the other disciples caused such a change in his life."

"I suppose not."

"The only thing that adequately explains Paul's conversion is that he really saw the risen Christ. And that's what he said was at the heart of his preaching. Look here at what he wrote in 1 Corinthians 15:

"'For I delivered to you first of all that which I also received: that Christ died for our sins according to the Scriptures, and that He was buried, and that He rose again the third day according to the Scriptures, and that He was seen by Cephas, then by the twelve. After that He was seen by over five hundred brethren at once, of whom the greater part remain to the present, but some have fallen asleep. After that He was seen by James, then by all the apostles. And last of all He was seen by me also. . . .'

"Does that sound like the words of somebody who got tricked by a made-up story?"

"No. I guess it doesn't make much sense to say the disciples made up the story."

"I don't think so."

"But what about the Jews and the Romans? Couldn't they have stolen the body?"

"What, and kept it hidden for months and then years, when parading it before the world would have destroyed the disciples' credibility and nipped Christianity in the bud?"

"I suppose not."

"And besides, that still wouldn't explain the eyewitness accounts by people who said they saw Jesus—particularly Paul, who was a 'hostile witness,' as lawyers put it today, until his encounter with the risen Christ."

"Okay, Jim. There's no way around the fact that the disciples and others saw Jesus after His crucifixion. But that doesn't prove He rose from the dead."

"Why not?"

"Because he might not have died on the cross. Suppose he'd just fainted—gone into shock maybe, and the soldiers *thought* he was dead, but he wasn't. Then, in the cool air of the cave he was buried in, he came out of shock, left the tomb, and later recovered."

"And . . . ?"

"And what?"

"And then what did He do?"

"Well, then He got together with his friends, and since

they'd thought He'd been dead before, naturally they thought that He'd come back to life."

"Naturally?"

"Why not?"

"What's so natural about coming back to life?"

"Nothing. But the disciples—"

"—were just as skeptical as you are, remember? And they didn't *expect* Him to rise from the dead—at least that's what they wrote later when they told their story."

"Well, they could have made that up to hide the fact that—" Dave paused for a moment. He wasn't sure where he was headed with this one.

"To hide what, Dave?"

"The fact that they had made up the story of the resurrection."

"But that's not what you're arguing for, Dave. You're arguing that they didn't make it up at all, but were confused and thought Jesus, recovered from shock, was Jesus risen from the dead. So even if they were confused, they were at least sincere. They wouldn't have thought to hide anything."

"Oh, I see."

"And besides, if they'd made up the story of their not expecting the resurrection, that would have been a lie inherent in their entire story. And people—"

"—don't die for what they know is a lie. Right. I see your point, Jim."

"And besides, from what you know of Jesus' integrity, do you really think He'd have let His disciples go on believing what *He* knew to be false?"

"No, I guess not."

"Not to mention that people in shock go deeper into shock in cool air; they don't come out of it. And that the soldiers thrust a spear through Jesus' side *after* they'd already judged Him dead, just to be sure they couldn't be mistaken. John says when they did that, blood and water—some clear liquid—rushed out together (John 19:34). The only good medical explanation for that is that the pericardium, the membrane that surrounds the heart, was broken. No one could have survived that plus the spear-pierced lungs plus the lethal rigors of crucifixion, which often killed victims in just a couple of hours' time."

"So there's no way Jesus survived the cross?"

"Right."

"But it's clear that He was seen alive later?"

"Seems pretty clear to me."

"So He rose from the dead?"

"Read the Gospels yourself, Dave, and judge the testimony for yourself."[10]

"I'm doing that. I've about finished Matthew."

"Great. Look, I've got to study for a history exam. Can we get together tomorrow night?"

"Sure, Jim. I'm enjoying this. I'm not sure I like where it's leading, but it just wouldn't be honest to ignore the evidence you're presenting."

Chapter 6

Is Jesus the Only Way to God?

The next evening found Dave back at Jim's apartment. He was eager but still wary. And he had some new questions in mind.

"Jim," he said, "an awful lot of what you've said is pretty persuasive. But something's troubling me."

"What's that, Dave?"

"I suppose the historical probabilities are strong that Jesus rose from the dead. I'll grant you that. But they're still only probabilities. They're not absolute proof. And if I understand you correctly, you're asking me to commit my life to Jesus. I can't do that. For that, I want absolute proof."

"That's pretty inconsistent, Dave."

"I don't think so. I think it's pretty consistent. I'm not gullible, after all."

"No, you're not. And I'm not asking you to be. I'm just asking you to apply the same criteria to this issue that you do to a great deal of other issues in your life."

"But this one is so much more important!"

"Really? I'll grant you, it's a life-or-death issue. But so are lots of other things in your life. Remember when we talked about different ways of knowing? I pointed out that you commit 100 percent of yourself to crossing the street, despite your not having 100 percent proof in advance that you'll make it across alive."

"I suppose so."

"And when you go up in an elevator, you don't have absolute proof that the cable won't break and send it crashing down, leaving you dead, do you?"

"No."

"But you don't leave 5 or 10 percent of yourself standing on one floor while the other goes up, do you?"

"No. But I don't have that choice there. It's all or nothing."

"And it's the same way with Jesus. All or nothing."

"I guess the two are pretty similar after all."

"Yes, they are. And remember what we said about the stakes in a decision influencing its direction?"

"Yes, I do. High stakes might sensibly lead us to decide one way even without strong evidence, if the other alternatives were even less supported."

"And yesterday you were saying that the evidence for Christ's resurrection was pretty strong, remember?"

"You're right."

"Dave, I've never said I could give you 100 percent proof of Christianity. But I think I've given you some very strong evidence—stronger than you have for believing a lot of other things, I'll bet. But even if those evidences weren't that strong, you'd have good reason to commit yourself to Jesus, because the stakes are so high. You have a great deal to lose if you don't and Christianity is true, and nothing to lose if you do and it's false. Jesus says if you reject Him, you'll die in your sins—condemned forever by God."

"But why couldn't there be some other way?"

"Why couldn't there? Well, I think there are some reasons why there *couldn't* be, but they involve some pretty complex theology. For the moment, it should be enough that Jesus says there *aren't* any other ways. 'I am the way, the truth, and the life,' He said. 'No one comes to the Father except through Me' (John 14:6)."

"But why should I believe that?"

"Because of who said it. If Jesus is God—and His resurrection gives pretty strong confirmation of His claims that He is—then whatever He says is true."

"But I still don't understand why there couldn't be other ways to God."

"Look, Dave, our sins put us under God's judgment. God is perfect, and He demands perfection in us. But none of us is perfect, so we can't meet His demands. Because God is just, He must punish sin. But Jesus said He came to give His life to ransom sinners from the penalty (Matthew 20:28)."

"Why couldn't God just accept us as we are—forgive us and have done with it?"

"Because He's holy and just, and our sins make us repugnant to Him. As Habakkuk, a Jewish prophet before Jesus, put it, 'You are of purer eyes than to behold evil, and cannot look on wickedness' (Habakkuk 1:13). Our sins separate us from God. There's nothing we can do about it ourselves. The very best we can do isn't perfect, and none of it can wipe away the debt we owe because of sin. Yet God's love for us is so strong that He promised, through the prophets, that He would send His Son to bear the punishment for sin as our substitute, so that we could be set free from sin and its punishment and be reconciled to God. Jesus fulfilled those promises."

Dave didn't answer. Jim let him sit quietly for a while, thinking. He was clearly having to weigh carefully what Jim was saying. Finally Jim went on.

"Dave, the price God paid to deliver us from punishment

for sin was infinitely precious—His own Son. If there had been any other way for us to reach God, Jesus wouldn't have had to die. That He did die shows that there was no other way salvation could be achieved. His resurrection proved He was who He said He was and that His death did what He said it did—it paid the penalty for our sins."

"All right, Jim," Dave said after another long pause. "I can hold that in abeyance for a while. Something else you just said interests me. You mentioned predictions in the Old Testament that Jesus fulfilled. How in the world can anyone foretell the future?"

"It isn't naturally possible, Dave. But the prophecies weren't natural. They were given by God."

"Give me a few examples, will you?"

"Sure. Over a thousand years before Jesus' birth, King David of Israel wrote prophetically that the Savior God would send would be crucified. In Psalm 22 he described in amazing detail what a crucifixion is like; yet the Romans didn't introduce crucifixion as a form of torture and execution until some eight hundred years later."

"You're saying he described a punishment that didn't exist?"

"Right. In great detail."

"Amazing."

"Over five hundred years before Jesus' birth, Zechariah, an Old Testament prophet, quoted God as predicting that He Himself would become a man and that His own people would kill Him (Zechariah 12:10). Isaiah predicted that the Savior would be born of a virgin (Isaiah 7:14)—a miracle impossible for any man to manufacture for himself—and Matthew reports that Jesus was indeed born of a virgin (Matthew 1:18-25)."

"Yes, I remember reading that a couple of days ago. But couldn't the people in those days just have been naive and believed in a virgin birth without good reason, not knowing it was impossible?"

"People like the skeptical disciples, Dave? Come on. Give 'em a break. They weren't gullible; you've seen that. And remember Mary's response when she was told she'd have a child? She couldn't believe it at first, because she'd never had intercourse with anyone."

"That's right. I read that in Luke last night."

"You're really moving through the Gospels, aren't you?"

"Well, since we've been having these conversations, they've become fascinating to me."

"I don't doubt it. They're the most fascinating stories I've ever read—and what makes them so great is that they're not just stories, they're true."

"Well, that's your view anyway. I'm not so sure. But get back to prophecies, will you?"

"Sure. Micah predicted that the Savior would be born in Bethlehem (Micah 5:2), and He was (Matthew 2:1). Jeremiah predicted that His birth would lead to the killing of infants throughout the area in which He was born (Jeremiah 31:15), and Herod had all male children two years old and under in Bethlehem and its surroundings killed in an attempt to kill Jesus (Matthew 2:16-18). Hosea predicted the Savior's trip into Egypt (Hosea 11:1). King David predicted that the Messiah would be betrayed by a friend (Psalms 41:9; 55:12-14), and He was (Matthew 10:4; 26:49-50; John 13:21).

"Zechariah predicted the price of the betrayal would be thirty pieces of silver (Zechariah 11:12), and it was (Matthew 26:15). He predicted the betrayer would throw the silver into the Temple in remorse (Zechariah 11:13), and Judas did (Matthew 27:5). He predicted the silver would be used to buy a potter's field (Zechariah 11:13), and it was (Matthew 27:7).

"David predicted that false witnesses would testify against Jesus (Psalm 35:11), and they did (Matthew 26:59-61).

Isaiah predicted that the Savior would be silent before His accusers (Isaiah 53:7), and He was (Matthew 27:12-14). He predicted that Jesus would be wounded and bruised for the sins of men (Isaiah 53), and He was (Matthew 27:26; 20:28); that He would be hit and spat upon (Isaiah 50:6), and He was (Matthew 26:67). David predicted that He would be mocked (Psalm 22:7-8), and He was (Matthew 27:29), and that His hands and feet would be pierced (Psalm 22:16), and they were when He was crucified. Isaiah predicted that He would be killed along with criminals (Isaiah 53:12), and He was (Matthew 27:38; Mark 15:27-28). Isaiah even predicted that the Savior would, while being killed by His own people, plead for God to forgive them (Isaiah 53:12), and Jesus did that (Luke 23:34)."

"Yes, I remember reading that last night, too. That really amazed me."

"Well, that's the love of Jesus, Dave. Pretty amazing, isn't it?"

"Yes, I think so."

"At any rate, Jesus fulfilled these and lots of other prophecies in the Old Testament. The odds against this happening were enormous. Imagine for a moment that there were only ten such prophecies, and that the chances were 50/50 on each one that anyone would fulfill them. (The chances were really much higher against it—especially on things like the virgin birth!) The odds against His fulfilling all ten would have been one in two to the tenth power, or one in 2,048. But there weren't only ten, there were some three hundred predictions of the coming Messiah, and Jesus fulfilled all of them. The odds? About one in two to the three hundredth power!"

"All right, all right. You've made the point."

"So what's the most reasonable explanation, Dave?"

"I suppose it's that the prophets got their predictions from God, and Jesus really fulfilled them."[11]

"So He really was who He said He was—God in human form. And He really died to pay for our sins. What you need to do now, Dave, is to trust in Him for forgiveness of your sins, commit yourself to Him."

"Hold on a minute, Jim. Not so fast. Some other questions have been occurring to me over the last couple of days. I've kept forgetting to bring them up in our conversations, we cover so much territory and go so fast. But last night I listed a few. I'd really like to see what you have to say about them."

"Can't guarantee I'll have answers to all of them, but I'll do my best."

"Okay. For starters, isn't Christianity just a crutch for weak people?"

"Yes and no. No, it isn't *just* that. But yes, it is that. But that doesn't make it untrue. People with broken legs need crutches. People with broken hearts need a spiritual crutch, something to get them up and walking. There's no shame in using a crutch when you need one."

"But I don't."

"Really? Then you're in a class by yourself, Dave. And you don't believe that. You told me before that you realized you had done some wrong things and not done some right things you should have done. Face it, friend, you're a sinner. God gave us moral laws, Dave, and the Bible says, 'Cursed is the one who does not confirm all the words of this law' (Deuteronomy 27:26). Paul agreed, writing, 'Cursed is everyone who does not continue in all things which are written in the book of the law, to do them' (Galatians 3:10). God requires perfection, Dave, and you don't measure up. You need this crutch as much as anybody else."

"But didn't God give the law to the Jews? It doesn't apply to anyone else, does it?"

"Paul says that the substance of that law is written in the heart of every person (Romans 2:14-15), which is why everyone is accountable to that law, whether we've ever seen it in writing or not. Come on, Dave. You know your own heart well enough to know that you've often done what you knew full well was wrong."

"I guess so. I just don't like having someone sit in judgment over me and call me a sinner."

"Well, Dave, I'm not sitting in judgment over you. You can do that well enough for yourself. But I am reminding you of what your judgment—and God's—is."

"All right. But you're focusing just on my faults. Don't my good works count for anything?"

"They would if God were grading on a scale, but He doesn't grade that way. He requires perfection, remember? Jesus said, '. . . you shall be perfect, just as your Father in heaven is perfect' (Matthew 5:48)."

"Yeah, I read that too. It seems pretty unreasonable to me."

"But you're in no position to make up the rules, are you?"

"I don't understand."

"Well, who makes up the rules in this life? You, or God? I mean, if you make up the rules, can you name just one universal rule—one rule that applies to everybody—that *you* made up?"

"No."

"Dave, the simple fact is that this is God's world, not yours or mine or anyone else's. He made it, and He made the rules. One of the rules He determined is that the reward for sin is death—spiritual death, separation from God (Romans 6:23)."

"But it's so unfair. Nobody can be perfect."

"You're wrong in saying God's unfair to require perfection of us. The Bible says God made us in His image (Genesis 1:26), to be like Him; that's what we're supposed to be. Our imperfection is our fault, not His. And the Bible also assures us that God is just and fair in everything He does. The prophet Zephaniah wrote, 'The Lord is righteous. . . . He will do no unrighteousness. Every morning He brings His justice to light; He never fails' (Zephaniah 3:5).

"But you're right in saying nobody's perfect. And that's why God provided a way for imperfect sinners to be reconciled to Him—through faith in His Son Jesus and His death on the cross to pay the penalty for our sins."

"But that's not fair either. Why should I have to believe in Jesus to be forgiven?"

"Why should you have to follow the instructions in assembling a machine to make it work? Why should you have to use the right codes to make your computer work? Are these things unfair? Of course not. You have to follow the instructions and use the right codes because the designers made the machines and the computers to work that way.

"God is your Designer, Dave. He has told you what you have to do to 'work right,' to meet His requirements. It's not unfair for Him to have told you so, so long as what He demands is possible. He gives you two options: either be perfect yourself, or believe in Jesus and be forgiven for your imperfections. If you don't want to believe in Jesus, you're free to try being perfect—although it's a little late now."

"Look, Jim, I know I admitted before that I sin. But I'm not all that bad. Really evil people like Stalin and Hitler I can understand God rejecting. But you yourself tell me God is a God of love. My sins are just little things. Surely He can overlook them."

"You might not take them seriously, but God does. You see, God doesn't consider how much damage an act causes to others. He considers what it says about your attitude toward Him. As your Creator, God deserves your absolute obedience. Your disobedience indicates that you don't honor Him as you ought, and that's something much more serious than simply telling a lie or cheating or stealing. That's why James, a brother of Jesus, wrote, '. . . whoever shall keep the whole law, and yet stumble in one point, he is guilty of all. For He who said, "Do not commit adultery," also said, "Do not murder." Now if you do not commit adultery, but you do murder, you have become a transgressor of the law' (James 2:10-11). Maybe you don't think your sins are so serious, but God does. He thinks they're serious enough to require the sacrifice of His Son to pay for them."

"But I don't disrespect God!"

"Hmmm. That's a pretty quick change from having denied His existence until a few weeks ago."

"But that wasn't disrespect, that was misunderstanding."

"Even misunderstanding can be blameworthy, you know."

"How's that?"

"When it's willful. And the Bible says that those who deny the existence of God do so in willful rejection of the obvious truth of His existence. The Apostle Paul says that when people deny God's existence, they 'suppress the truth in unrighteousness, because what may be known of God is manifest in them, for God has shown it to them' (Romans 1:18-19)."

"But that's not true. It wasn't obvious to me before that God existed."

"Wasn't it? It should have been. Think again about the stuff we discussed—entropy, design, all that. If you stumbled across a fine, luxurious watch lying out in a field somewhere, you wouldn't assume it got there by chance, would you? You'd wonder where it came from, and you'd know instantly that whoever designed and made it was an intelligent and careful worker.

"Now think of yourself. You're a lot more intricately designed than any watch ever made—or any computer, either. Yet you used to think you came about by accident. You'd never excuse that willful ignorance in someone if he said it about a watch. Why should God excuse it in you when you said it about yourself? Sounds pretty disrespectful to me."

"I never thought of it that way before."

"Well, that's what the Bible says, and if you ask me, it makes perfect sense. That's why Paul went on to write, 'For since the creation of the world His invisible attributes are clearly seen, being understood by the things that are made, even His eternal power and Godhead, so that they are without excuse, because, although they knew God, they did not glorify Him as God, nor were thankful, but became futile in their thoughts, and their foolish hearts were darkened. Professing to be wise, they became fools . . .' (Romans 1:20-22)."

"So now you're calling me a fool?"

"Well, you were when you denied the existence of God. And if you're honest with yourself now, you'll admit that. And a willful fool at that. How else can you explain your failure to recognize that the intricate design in you bespoke an awesome Designer?"

"I guess I can't. Man, I have been a fool, haven't I?"

"You said it. But you're in good company. So has everyone else. Fools for disbelieving in God. Fools for thinking they could live successful, happy lives while flouting His laws. Fools for thinking they could make up for their sins with a few good deeds. Fools for rejecting God's perfectly wonderful, gracious offer of forgiveness to anyone who trusts in Jesus. Now's your chance to stop being a fool, Dave. Jesus said, 'For God so loved the world that He gave His only begotten Son, that whoever believes in Him should not perish, but have everlasting life. For God did not send His Son into the world to condemn the world, but that the world through Him might be saved' (John 3:16-17). Believe in Him, Dave."

"Okay, okay. I'm coming close, I think. But I still have some reservations."

"Such as?"

"Well, for one thing, you're saying Jesus is the only way to God. But don't all religions teach basically the same thing?"

"Not really. Other religions are primarily philosophies of life. In their moral codes, they're generally pretty similar to Christianity. But they don't offer any solution to our guilt for failing to live up to the moral code. Christianity, too, gives us a philosophy of life—a more full and reasonable and beautiful and intelligent one, I might add, than any other alternative— but it gives us one crucial thing more: a way to be reconciled to the God we've offended by our disbelief and disobedience. Most important, Christianity is Jesus; no other religion has Him."

"How do you know Christianity is true and the others are false?"

"One way to find out would be to examine all the other religions to see if they are logically consistent and correspond with reality. That would take years. (And I'm confident what the answer would be in each case, too.) But there's a faster way."

"What's that?"

"You've already done a good deal of it."

"How?"

"You've examined some of the evidences for the truth of Christianity—particularly that Christ is who He said He is. If you conclude that Christianity is true, then at every point at which any other religion contradicts Christianity, that religion must be false. The law of non-contradiction tells us that."

"Fair enough. But do they really contradict the essence of Christianity?"

"Of course. They deny that Jesus is God; they deny that faith in Him is the only way to be forgiven for sin and to be reconciled to God. They deny that Jesus died for our sins and rose again from the dead. That's the heart of Christianity. If Christianity's true, the other religions have to be false."

"But that's awfully intolerant. Why can't you be more tolerant of other religions?"

"It's not a question of toleration. Christianity says every person is free to worship God, or not worship Him, as he sees fit. It doesn't believe anyone should be—or can be—forced to believe in Christianity."

"But you do insist that only Christianity is true."

"Yes, but that's no more intolerant than insisting that whoever says two plus two equals anything but four is wrong. Toleration isn't a matter of what's true, but of what's permitted. Christians permit people to believe as they wish; they just say that some beliefs are false and others are true, and that the false beliefs will lead to a disastrous end."

"Isn't Islam compatible with Christianity? I've heard that Muhammad, who founded Islam, believed he was simply teaching pure Christianity."

"He might have thought so, but Jesus claimed to be God, and Muhammad denied that. Obviously he wasn't teaching the Christianity of Jesus. The Bible teaches that God is three Persons—Father, Son, and Holy Spirit, what we call the doctrine of the Trinity. Muhammad denied that."

"Why not believe Muhammad instead?"

"Well, we've already been through an awful lot of reasons to believe Jesus is who He said He is. What Christianity believes about Jesus comes from His own words about Himself and from the words of His closest followers. Muhammad's words about Jesus came some six hundred years later. Which would you have more confidence in?"

"Fair enough. But what was this 'Trinity' thing you mentioned? Are you telling me you believe in three gods?"

"No, not at all. The Bible tells us in many places that there is only one God (Deuteronomy 6:4; Isaiah 43:10; 1

Corinthians 8:6; 1 Timothy 2:5). But it also tells us that three Persons are the same God—the Father (John 17:3; 1 Corinthians 8:6; 1 Peter 1:2), the Son—Jesus Christ (John 1:1; 20:28; Philippians 2:6-7, compared with John 5:18; Titus 2:13; 2 Peter 1:1), and the Holy Spirit (Acts 5:3-4; Hebrews 9:14)."

"But that sounds illogical to me. How can three persons be one God?"

"I'll admit it sounds unusual. But it's not illogical. We're not used to seeing human beings who are more than one person, but that doesn't make it impossible for one being to be two or three or more persons. It just makes it strange so far as our own experience is concerned. The key is to remember that being and personhood are different kinds of things."

"What do you mean?"

"Look around you. You see lots of beings—a rock here, a tree there, a building over there, a cow out in the field. They're all beings, but they're not persons at all. But you also see some beings who are persons—every man, woman, and child you see is both a being and a person. So some beings are no persons, and other beings are one person. Nothing tells us no beings can be more than one person. And the Bible tells us that God *is* more than one person; He's three Persons. So long as you remember the difference between being and person, while it may seem strange to think of a single being as three persons, you can recognize that it isn't illogical. And it's because God is Father, Son, and Holy Spirit that Jesus instructed His disciples to baptize people into Christianity 'in the name of the Father and of the Son and of the Holy Spirit' (Matthew 28:19)."[12]

"It may not be illogical, but it sure is hard to understand."

"Shouldn't you expect many things about God to be hard to understand? After all, He has more power and intelligence than all the universe, and you don't exactly understand everything about that either, do you?"

"I guess you're right. But I do have another problem."

"What's that?"

"What about people who never hear of Christianity? Does God condemn them just for that?"

"Why do you ask, Dave?"

"Because if Christianity says God automatically rejects all who haven't heard of Jesus, I don't think it's worth believing."

"Why not? Would that contradict the evidences you've heard?"

"No."

"Then what's the problem?"

"I guess I just don't think I could worship a God who would be so unfair as to condemn people just because they never heard of Jesus."

"Good. It's important to recognize that your question doesn't have anything to do with the *truth* of Christianity, but with whether you are willing to *acknowledge* its truth and worship God. And your question says something good about you: you care about people other than yourself. That's called love, and God loves people, too. The Bible says God waits patiently for people (2 Peter 3:9) and that He's ready to show Himself to anyone who sincerely wants to know Him (John 7:17). What you can be sure of is that God's judgment is always fair and just (Acts 17:31). He would never send anyone to hell unjustly.

"In fact, God has gone out of His way to bring the news about Jesus to people who sincerely sought after Him. Luke tells us, in Acts 10, about a man named Cornelius who asked God to reveal Himself to him and show him whatever was necessary for salvation. God answered Cornelius's prayer by sending Peter to tell him about Jesus. When Peter told him, Cornelius believed. Maybe, Dave, that's what's happening now. God's answering your heartfelt desire to know Him by giving you this opportunity to hear about Jesus from me."

"Maybe. But what about the others?"

"If you really care about them, Dave, you won't use them

97

as an excuse to reject Jesus. Instead, you'll commit yourself to Jesus and then get busy telling them about Him, too."

"I have to admit, Jim, you make a strong case. Let me think on it some more."

"Sure, Dave."

Chapter 7

Why Would a Loving God Send Anyone to Hell?

Jim was sitting alone in the library, thinking to himself. *Why does Dave avoid me every time he sees me now? For three weeks, I've barely gotten anything more than a muttered "Hello" out of him. Last Monday he actually got up from a cafeteria table with a half-full tray and left, just to avoid having me sit down beside him. Something's wrong. I guess I got too rough on him that night in my apartment, when I called him a fool. Maybe I shouldn't have come on so strong.*

He'd gone over their conversations again and again in his mind, wondering where it was he'd made the wrong turn, where he'd crossed the line from friend to accuser. He wished he had a chance to do it all over again and say some things differently.

If only I'd let him save face, even just a little, Jim thought. *But now he doesn't even want to be around me. Lord, I've really blown it this time. Please do something to soothe Dave's heart and make him willing to talk again.*

Two more weeks went by. Dave kept on avoiding Jim,

and Jim became all the more convinced that he'd ruined what had seemed like a golden opportunity to share the gospel. This morning, like so many other mornings lately, the papers spread before him on the library table failed to hold his attention.

"Jim, let's talk."

The voice from behind was so unexpected, Jim jumped in surprise.

"I'm sorry I've been avoiding you all this time, Jim. I just—I didn't like what you said the last time we talked. We've always stayed on such a theoretical level. Last time you got personal, and what you said about me wasn't exactly complimentary . . . Calling me a fool, a willful fool, saying I disrespected God . . . Although I was offended when you said it, it all seemed to make sense at the time. I couldn't see a way around it. It's been eating at me ever since, and I've been thinking it through again and again. It made me pretty upset. That's why I've avoided talking to you."

"I was afraid of that," Jim said. "And I want to apologize—"

"No, no . . . Don't do that. It's not necessary."

"But, Dave, I mean it. I'm really sorry I got so intense and personal."

"Don't back off now, Jim. You see, ever since the last time we talked, I've stopped reading the Bible. I just didn't like what you told me, and I figured I'd just get more of the same there. But last night I started again, reading Romans, and I came to those verses you quoted—"

"About people suppressing the truth in unrighteousness and becoming fools because they refused to honor God?"

"Right. And you know what? They're true. I took a good, long, hard look at myself, and I realized what you said about me was true. Offensive, hard-hitting, but true. I don't like it, but I'm glad you had the guts to say it."

"Well, Dave, I want you to know that I really never meant

to offend you by it. I was just trying to answer your questions as honestly as I could."

"No problem, Jim. Look, I haven't become a Christian or anything, but I really want to continue with our conversations. I've got some more questions I hope you can help me work through."

"Sure, Dave. And this time I'll try to be a little more sensitive about how I answer."

"Well, do whatever you think is best. But I'm after truth, not warm fuzzies."

"All right. Thanks."

"First off, last time we talked, you mentioned hell. Now, if I understand rightly, you believe that's a place where people who don't believe in Christ suffer for eternity?"

"Yes."

"And you really believe in that?"

"Yes, I do, because Jesus said it exists. He taught that there will be a day of judgment for all people, and that on that day those who trust Him for the forgiveness of their sins will be granted entry into a joyous eternity in the presence of God, while those who reject Him will 'go away into everlasting punishment' (Matthew 25:46)."

"I don't remember that particular verse, but I do remember noticing when I read the Gospels that Jesus talked a great deal about hell. I have a tough time with that. How could a loving God let anyone go to hell? Any God who would do that couldn't be good."

"Why not?"

"Well, to torture people forever? Come on, Jim. That's not just. It's out of all proportion to what they've done."

"Is it really?"

"I think so."

"And what have they done?"

"Oh, they've done various things wrong, I admit that. But nothing to compare with eternal suffering."

"And against whom did they do those things?"

"Other people, of course."

"Is that all?"

"What do you mean?"

"Aren't you forgetting someone else they've sinned against?"

"Oh, well, yes . . . God, but—"

"Doesn't He count in your calculation of what's fitting punishment for people's sins?"

"What do you mean?"

"Well, you know how in some states there's a tougher sentence if you kill a policeman than for any other murder?"

"Yes."

"Why are the laws that way?"

"Because, I suppose, killing a policeman means not just attacking one person but the whole authority of the state and the society."

"Right. So the act itself isn't the only thing we consider when determining the sort of punishment a crime deserves. The status of the one against whom the crime is committed is relevant, too?"

"Yes, I think that's right."

"Think about it, Dave. When people sin against God, what level of authority do they defy?"

"If God is who you say He is, the highest, I guess."

"Right. And what degree of purity do they offend?"

"I'm not sure I follow you."

"Look, when someone lies to me, I can be offended, but I can't be very self-righteous about it. I've lied plenty of times in my life, too, right? So I can't be too judgmental. But when somebody sins against God, he sins against Someone infinitely perfect and holy."

"So you're saying he deserves great punishment because God Himself is so great?"

"Essentially, yes. And that ties in not only to the reality of hell—eternal torment—but also to the sacrifice of Christ."

"How's that?"

"Because our sins are against a God of infinite holiness, they are of infinite consequence. So the proper punishment for them is infinite. Now, we're finite, so we can't experience infinite punishment in a finite period of time; it takes eternity for us to experience infinite punishment. God planned for someone to bear our punishment as our substitute, but whoever would do it would have to be capable of bearing infinite punishment in a finite time. That's why the substitute had to be infinite Himself; that's why the Son of God became a man, so that as a man He could properly represent those for whom He died, and as God His payment could be infinite, enough to satisfy the justice of God's infinite holiness."

"From that angle, it sounds sensible, but it sure bugs me."

"I'm not saying I *like* the doctrine of hell. It's no fun to contemplate having people I've loved spend eternity in torment. But either I acknowledge it, or I deny Jesus, because Jesus taught frequently about hell. I can't deny Jesus; the evidence is too strong that He is who He claimed to be. So I've got to accept hell."

"I don't know, Jim. It just doesn't fit my idea of a loving God."

"Look, think of it this way . . . True, God says those who reject Christ will go to hell. But *He does offer them Christ, freely and openly*. To put it rather simply, for me it's more difficult to understand how a holy and just and good God could allow anyone to go to heaven, when everyone deserves to go to hell because everyone has sinned against Him."

"So you're saying that what should shock us is not that anyone is lost but that anyone is saved?"

"Yes. Hell, after all, is only what we *deserve*. Heaven is the great gift. If you have any doubts about God being loving and gracious and compassionate, consider that while He could justly have written us all off, instead He paid the debt for sin and promised that anyone who admits he's a sinner, is sorry for his sin, and trusts in Jesus to forgive his sin will be saved."

"That does kind of turn things around, doesn't it?" Dave thought for a minute. "But I still don't like it."

"Do you like knowing that hurricanes sometimes level hundreds of homes and kill scores of people at a single swipe?"

"Of course not, but what's that got to do with it?"

"You don't deny the reality of hurricanes just because you don't like them, do you?"

"No. I see what you mean."

"Listen, Dave. If you're so concerned about people going to hell, do something about it. Give your life to Christ and then tell others about Him. Otherwise, your concern about God's goodness loses a lot of credibility. After all, He sacrificed His Son to keep people out of hell. What have you done that compares with that?"

"All right. Point well taken. But, Jim, why, if the evidence for Christianity is so good—and I'm beginning to see now that it is—why are there so few Christians?"

"What's that got to do with it?"

"It just seems to me that if Christianity were true, more people would believe in it."

"Would that make a difference in your decision?"

"Some, yes."

"That surprises me. I thought you were more of an independent thinker than that, Dave."

"I am, but—"

"But what, Dave?"

"But it just doesn't make sense that there are so few Christians if it has such a persuasive case."

"Few relative to what?"

"Well, relative to the whole world, I guess."

"And do you know what percentage of the world's people profess the Christian faith?"

"Oh, I don't know."

"About a third. And two thousand years ago less than one in a million did. That seems like pretty decent growth to me. And Christianity is growing explosively right now in places like Africa, Asia, Latin America, and the former Communist countries. Does that affect your thinking?"

"A little bit, I guess."

"You surprise me again. Really, Dave, what are you doing? Judging truth by popular vote?"

"No, Jim. Well, I guess you're right. There was an element of that in my thinking. Still, if a third of the world's people claim to be Christians, that leaves two thirds who don't. Why do so many reject Christianity?"

"You might be a better person to answer that question than I am, Dave. After all, I'm the Christian here; you're not. So why aren't you?"

"Because I'm not sure Christianity's true."

"Fine. And that's probably why lots of other people aren't Christians. Of course, too, lots have never heard of it, some have mistaken ideas of what it is—"

"Yeah, I guess I did, too, until the last few months."

"Sure, because you'd never taken the time to really study it carefully."

"Right. I had the idea that Christianity was a bunch of do's and don'ts. Mostly don'ts."

"That's what a lot of people think. But in reality, Christianity is real freedom—freedom from the sin that holds us captive until we trust Jesus as Savior and Lord, freedom from the condemnation and guilt that we deserve because of our sin, freedom from the feeling we have to perform up to a certain standard to please God."

"But don't we?"

"Like I said before, God gives us two options: 'Be perfect, as I'm perfect, or trust in Christ to be your substitute.'"

"Are you saying that anybody who believes in Jesus can just go on living whatever way he wants?"

"No, not at all. I'm saying that a changed, pure life isn't how we get into a right relationship with God; it's the *result* of a right relationship with God. We can't be that way before we're converted, because we're slaves to sin. After we're converted, we're set free and God gives us the strength to begin living the way we're meant to live."

"Jim, the more I listen to you, the more I'd like to be a Christian. But—"

Dave was hesitating. He didn't seem to know how to say what was on his mind.

"What is it, Dave?"

"It's a little embarrassing."

"So? You've done some things you're not proud of. Does that make you different from everybody else?"

"But I'm not talking about small stuff, Jim. You haven't known me for very long."

"A couple of years, I guess."

"Right. And in these couple of years you haven't always been around me. I've done some pretty rotten things in my life."

"And you're wondering whether God can forgive you for them?"

"Yes." Dave was silent for a long while. Finally he spoke again. "In high school I got my girlfriend, Anna, pregnant. She was pretty shook up, but she wanted to keep the baby. I made her get an abortion because I didn't want to be responsible for the kid. I felt like an ogre doing it. I swore I'd never do it again.

But just last spring I got Marcy pregnant, and I did the same terrible thing! I feel so guilty, I could kill myself, Jim! And I'm afraid it might happen with Sarah."

"Dave, I'm not going to minimize the seriousness of what you've done. You've committed adultery and pushed two girls into killing their babies. So far as God's concerned, you're an adulterer and a murderer."

"You see, Jim? I can't drag those things to Jesus and just say, 'Here, forgive me for these. Sorry.'"

"Maybe, maybe not. If you really didn't care, if you weren't truly sorry, He'd know your heart, and all your words would mean nothing. But the Bible says, in Psalm 51:17, 'The sacrifices of God are a broken spirit, a broken and a contrite heart—these, O God, You will not despise.'"

"Man, my heart is broken, all right."

"Dave, do you know who wrote those words?"

"No."

"A man with the same name as yours."

"David?"

"Right. And what really makes them fitting for your situation is when he wrote them."

"When was that, Jim?"

"Well, David was king, remember? And once he sent his armies out to battle, but he stayed back at the palace. From there he saw a woman bathing, naked, on her rooftop. Her name was Bathsheba. He fell for her, hard, and as king it wasn't difficult to get her. So he had an affair with her. She got pregnant while her husband was away with the army. David knew that even though he was king, he was subject to the law against adultery in Israel, so—"

"Really? He couldn't just pull rank?"

"Pull rank on God? Not hardly! No, Dave, God's laws apply equally to all people everywhere, high and low, rich and poor, weak and powerful. At any rate, David figured if

Bathsheba's husband, Uriah, came home and found her far along in her pregnancy, he'd know he wasn't the father, and one thing would lead to another, and David would at least lose his reputation, if not his throne. So first he arranged for Uriah to be given leave early in the pregnancy, so he could sleep with his wife and he'd think later he was the baby's father. But that didn't work. Uriah was too loyal to his fellow soldiers; he refused to sleep with his wife while they were on the field of battle. So David ordered that Uriah be sent to the front lines and then abandoned in the heat of battle—a sure way to get him killed. The officers carried out the orders, and Uriah was killed."

"So what happened?"

"A while later, the prophet Nathan came to David and confronted him with his sin. Like you, David—when he realized what he'd really done—was brokenhearted. But unlike you—at least until recently—King David knew how great God's love and mercy are, and he knew that he could find forgiveness in God. So he wrote a prayer confessing his sin, asking for forgiveness, and promising to live for God after that. Psalm 51 is that prayer—a song, really." Jim picked his Bible up from the stack of books on the table. "Here, look with me at what it says:

> "'Have mercy upon me, O God, according to Your loving-kindness; according to the multitude of Your tender mercies, blot out my transgressions. Wash me thoroughly from my iniquity, and cleanse me from my sin. For I acknowledge my transgressions, and my sin is always before me—'"

"Well, he wasn't denying his guilt, was he?" Dave said.
"No, he wasn't.

"'. . . my sin is always before me. Against You, You only, have I sinned, and done this evil in Your sight—that You may be found just when You speak, and blameless when You judge.

"'Behold, I was brought forth in iniquity, and in sin my mother conceived me. Behold, You desire truth in the inward parts, and in the hidden part You will make me to know wisdom. Purge me with hyssop—'"

"What's that all about?"

"Well, in one ceremony signifying the forgiveness of sins and the cleansing of people's hearts, the priests of Israel used to use branches of hyssop to sprinkle people, symbolizing a washing process."

"Okay. Go on."

"'Purge me with hyssop, and I shall be clean; wash me, and I shall be whiter than snow. Make me hear joy and gladness, that the bones You have broken may rejoice. Hide Your face from my sins, and blot out all my iniquities.

"'Create in me a clean heart, O God, and renew a steadfast spirit within me. Do not cast me away from Your presence, and do not take Your Holy Spirit from me. Restore to me the joy of Your salvation, and uphold me by Your generous Spirit. Then I will teach transgressors Your ways, and sinners shall be converted to You.

"'Deliver me from the guilt of bloodshed, O God, the God of my salvation, and my tongue shall sing aloud of Your righteousness. O Lord, open my lips, and my mouth shall show forth Your praise. For You do not desire sacrifice, or else I would give it; You do not delight in burnt offering. The sacrifices of God are a broken spirit, a broken and a contrite heart—These, O God, You will not despise.'

"You see, Dave, King David was really an awful lot like you. He, too, committed adultery. He, too, murdered some-body—or rather, like you, got somebody else to do the killing for him. But he went sincerely to God, sorry for his sins, and found forgiveness there. And he went on to be the greatest king Israel ever had. In fact, the Bible even calls him a 'man after God's own heart.' You can have that forgiveness, too, Dave."

"Boy, Jim, it's hard. I want it so bad I can taste it. But I'm just not sure. Give me some more time."

"I can't force you, buddy. You'll never believe until *you* believe."

"Yeah. You're right."

Dave looked away for a while. Jim thought it best not to push right now. Dave's confessions had taken a lot out of him.

Finally Dave spoke. It wasn't what Jim hoped to hear. "Later, Jim. I need to do some thinking alone." He walked out of sight.

Chapter 8

Why Should I Believe the Bible?

Jim was afraid Dave would start avoiding him again. He'd probably be embarrassed about what he'd confessed. But he was wrong. Dave might have been embarrassed, but he was also determined to get some things resolved. He came to Jim's apartment the very next day.

"Jim," he said, "I really appreciate your attitude yesterday. You could have come down hard on me for what I've done, but you didn't. You didn't make light of it, but you didn't condemn me either."

"Why should I, Dave? I'm no better than you are."

"You mean you've—"

"Gotten girls pregnant and pushed them to get abortions? No. But I fall just as far short of God's infinite perfection as you do. I'm just one sinner saved by the grace of God pointing the way for another sinner to be saved by the grace of God."

"Well, anyway, thanks. But you know, one thing that bothers me is that you constantly turn to the Bible for answers to my questions."

"That's because it's God's Word, Dave. It's got the answers."

"*You* believe it's God's Word, but I don't."

"You should, though."

"Why?"

"Well, for a variety of reasons. For instance, Jesus believed it was. He never questioned the truth of the Old Testament—the part of the Bible that existed during His life here on earth. He always assumed it. John 10 tells us that He actually called it the Word of God."

"The Old Testament, maybe. But what about the New?"

"Jesus promised the disciples that the Holy Spirit would so guide their thoughts that they would remember perfectly all He had taught them, so that they could pass it along to others (John 14:26). They apparently understood Him to mean that their writings would be on a level with the Old Testament. Peter, for instance, put Paul's writings on that level (2 Peter 3:15-16), and Paul consistently claimed that his teaching and writing were God's words (1 Corinthians 7:40; 1 Thessalonians 2:13). He described the Old Testament as 'God-breathed' (2 Timothy 3:16), and Jesus' promise to the disciples indicates that their writings would be equally of divine origin."

"But you see, Jim, you're quoting the Bible to prove the Bible. That's circular reasoning."

"No, it isn't. Because when I quote the Bible to prove the Bible, I'm not quoting it as God's Word. I'm just quoting it as what we already agree it is—a generally reliable historical document."

"So what's the difference?"

"The difference is that I'm not arguing in a circle, but in a straight line."

"I don't follow you."

"The New Testament, which we already know is historically reliable, gives solid evidence that Jesus rose from the dead, proving Himself God. If He was God, then whatever He says is true. The New Testament also gives solid evidence that Jesus said the Bible is God's Word. If He said it, then it's true."

"So you're saying that if Jesus was who He said He was, there's no avoiding the conclusion that the Bible is true?"

"Right."

"Let me see if I've got your argument straight. If I understand you, it would have five points. First, the New Testament is a reliable historical document. Second, it gives us strong evidence that Jesus is God. Third, if Jesus is God, then He's an infallible authority. Fourth—well, how's it go from there?"

"Fourth, according to the New Testament, Jesus considered the Bible God's Word."

"Yeah. And fifth, if the Bible is God's Word, then it's all true, because God doesn't lie."

"Precisely. I couldn't have put it better myself."

"So in essence, we have as much reason to believe the Bible is God's Word as to believe that Jesus is God?"[13]

"Right."

"Okay, I can see the strength of that argument. But I'm still not convinced."

"Well, let me give you a few more reasons to take the Bible seriously. First, the Bible is unique. It was written over a period of fifteen hundred years by more than forty authors in three languages on three continents. Its authors included high government officials, peasants, military officers, fishermen, religious teachers, and various others. It purports to tell us of the beginning and end of the world. It claims to be God's Word—a claim made by few other writings and substantiated by none others. It has survived innumerable attempts to destroy it.

"Second, the Bible is unified. Although it speaks on hundreds of controversial topics, it never contradicts itself—a tough order even for a single book by a single author! And its unity includes more than non-contradiction. From beginning to end, there's one unfolding story of God's plan of salvation through Jesus Christ. The Old Testament prepares us for Christ's coming, the Gospels tell of His life, the Book of Acts tells of the early spread of the good news about His life and death and resurrection, the letters of Paul, Peter, James, John, and others explain the good news and elucidate Jesus' teachings, and the Book of Revelation tells us about the end of the world and Jesus' triumph over all evil. The whole Bible is about Jesus. I think this unity is beyond man's capacity to produce. It indicates that someone else did it—God.

"Third, the Bible has enormous power to change lives. Throughout history, people who have embraced Christ and begun to live by the Bible have been transformed in ways otherwise unimaginable. And so have whole civilizations."

"But none of these things really *proves* the Bible to be God's Word."

"True. I think they attest to its power, but you're right. They don't prove it's God's Word."

"So why should I believe it?"

"For one thing, because the preponderance of evidence points that way. For another, because the stakes are high; you've got a lot to gain and nothing to lose from believing it. But most important, because God Himself says, in the Bible, that the Bible is His Word. You'll either accept that or not, but whether you do won't have any effect on the truth of it."

"Wait a minute. You claim the Bible is unified. But I've heard that the Old Testament presents God as vengeful and hateful, demanding justice, while the New Testament describes Him as gracious, loving, and forgiving."

"Lots of people think that. But the Old Testament teaches God's love and grace just as strongly as the New, and the New Testament teaches God's justice and wrath against sin just as strongly as the Old."

"Give me some examples."

"Well, you yourself pointed out how much the Gospels quote Jesus talking about hell."

"But what about grace and love in the Old Testament?"

"There's Psalm 51 to begin with—what we read yesterday morning. And Ezekiel 18 quotes God as saying He has no pleasure in the death of the wicked but would rather he turned from his ways and lived. And one of the most important descriptions of God comes in Exodus 34, where God reveals Himself to Moses as 'The Lord, the Lord God, merciful and gracious, longsuffering, and abounding in goodness and truth, keeping mercy for thousands, forgiving iniquity and transgression and sin, by no means clearing the guilty. . . .'"

"I think I understand. In fact, right there God describes Himself as both just and loving."

"Right, which is why there's such a thing as hell and yet also the offer of free salvation through Jesus."

"I see."

Jim didn't expect what came next.

"You mind going back to a subject we touched on a long time ago—a couple of months ago, in fact—but didn't get back to?"

"No, go ahead."

"Well, you remember when we were talking about whether the universe was created, and I brought up evolution?"

"Yes."

"You said we could talk about evolution later."

"Fine. What about it?"

"Well, doesn't the Bible contradict science when it comes to evolution?"

"It contradicts some scientists, yes, but that's not the same thing as contradicting science itself."

"What's the difference?"

"Scientists believe all kinds of different things. They disagree with each other. Some believe in a big bang, some in a steady state universe, some in a pulsating universe. Some believe in gradual, Darwinian evolution, some in punctuated equilibrium, some in the creation of specific kinds of life by God. Some of the latter believe in a relatively recent creation, others in creation billions of years ago. Some scientists believe in general relativity, others in spatial particle theory. Some believe in black holes, and some don't. Since scientists disagree on so many issues—many of them pretty basic—I hardly think it's a problem for the Bible to disagree with some of them on some things."

"But evolution's different, Jim. All scientists agree on that. They might disagree about exactly how it happened, but they agree that it did."

"Back to determining truth by majority—even unanimous—vote, Dave?"

"Well, no, but these are qualified scientists."

"True. And so are the thousands of scientists worldwide who are members of the Creation Research Society and who believe evolution is a myth not supported by sound scientific evidence."

"The *what* society?"

"The Creation Research Society, whose members hold Ph.D.'s in various hard sciences and believe the rest of the scientific community is mistaken about evolution."

"I never heard of them."

"Well, they're there. In fact, I've got some copies of the *Creation Research Society Quarterly* in a file cabinet over there. You're welcome to borrow some if you'd like."

"Thanks. But why do they deny evolution? Just because they believe the Bible?"

"I can tell you a few of their reasons. Then I can lend you some books in which you can read more. I'm not a specialist in this field myself, so you'll get better information from them."

"All right."

"First, let's make sure we've defined our terms properly. Creationists don't deny micro-evolution—variation within basic life forms. What they deny is macro-evolution—change from one basic kind of life to another."

"So they don't think God created every different variety of cat, for instance, but that He did create cats and dogs?"

"Right. Now, there's lots of scientific evidence for micro-evolution. But for macro-evolution? Not much. It's more a philosophy than a science. Even its proponents acknowledge that it can't be proved by experiment or observation and that many parts of the theory—such as the idea of natural selection—are so vaguely defined as to be completely untestable and therefore not strictly scientific."

"Yeah, I remember being bothered by that in a biology course I took in undergraduate school. We talked about natural selection, and the idea was that it meant that the fittest survived, but how you defined the fittest was simply whichever survived. Sounded illogical—like circular reasoning—to me then, and it still does."

"That's because it is. Another problem is that macro-evolution contradicts the law of entropy."

"How?"

"What is the principle of entropy?"

"That matter and energy tend toward randomness, available energy decreases in a closed system, things tend naturally from order to disorder, not vice versa."

"Exactly. And in contrast, what does evolution say happened, purely by chance?"

"Oh, yes." Dave's expression changed as the contradiction began to dawn on him. "I see what you're getting at. Evolution says things go from less order to greater, from simple to complex."

"Right. And it makes that claim not only for living systems, which have their own internal ordering mechanism—DNA—but also for non-living systems, which they say gave birth to the first life purely by chance combinations of chemicals."

"I'd never thought of that contradiction before."

"Neither have most evolutionists. It's amazing to me how foolish the notion of abiogenesis—life from non-life—is. After all, here are all these biochemists trying desperately to synthesize life in their laboratories. They use complex computer programs, they carefully control all the conditions, and they can't synthesize life. The closest they can come is to take apart something living and then try to put it back together. And yet they say life originated by chance."

"About as foolish as my not recognizing that the intricate design in my own mind and body were testimony of a Creator/Designer. I see. But then, odds that might seem impossible over a short time could be otherwise over a long time."

"Theoretically, yes. But in fact, the various steps, the building blocks, of life are themselves incredibly complex, and their chance formation is incredibly unlikely. And they would have no advantage in chemical survival unconnected with the rest of the building blocks. So in fact, adding time as a factor doesn't really make any difference."

"I see what you're talking about. It's like the odds of getting heads on any given flip of the coin are still 50/50 no matter how many times in a row you've already gotten heads."

"Right. But I'm not really an expert in these things. Here . . . You might be interested in reading this book by Sir Fred Hoyle and N. Chandra Wickramasinghe—*Evolution from Space: A Theory of Cosmic Creationism.*[14] Now, Hoyle and Wickramasinghe aren't Christians that I know of—at least, they weren't when they wrote this—and in general they still accepted the idea of evolution once life began. But they're world-class astrophysicists and mathematicians, and what they knew of probability and statistics convinced them that the chance formation of even the most elementary building block of life—a single amino acid—was, as they put it, about as likely as a tornado blowing through a junkyard and assembling a Boeing 747."

"I'll read this for sure. Hoyle's a big name in astrophysics."

"I think you'll enjoy it. By the way, the dogmatic evolutionists have largely ostracized Hoyle and Wickramasinghe because of this book."

"So much for objective scientists! My science professors always made a big deal of how back in the Middle Ages the Christian Church used to persecute scientists whose theories went against the Church's ideas. It sounds like today's scientists are doing the same thing."

"They are. The scientific community has its own orthodoxy and heresy, and its own witch trials, today. The Church did some of that in the past, although probably less than many people think. And in fact, most of the great scientists of the past were Christians who studied science because they believed they were studying God's handiwork."[15]

"Okay, but that has to do with how life began. What about how it developed? You say Hoyle and this other fellow—what's his name?"

"Wickramasinghe. He's from Sri Lanka."

"Anyway, they reject the chance formation of the first life. But what about after that?"

"Same problems. How is life supposed to have evolved?"

"By mutation through natural selection is what I've always been taught."

"Right. And you've just pointed out how logically empty the idea of natural selection is."

"True. But mutations are for real. We can see them happening."

"Right. But tell me something. Have you ever heard of a bunch of scientists marching in protest against safety measures that prevent the release of radiation from nuclear power plants?"

"Of course not! That would be crazy. And what does it have to do with evolution anyway?"

"Nothing much, except that radiation is the most effective way to cause mutations, and if mutations are supposed to be the wonderful things that drive evolution, why not get more of them?"

"Well . . . Good question!" Dave was starting to get pretty agitated. "Evolutionists really are inconsistent, aren't they?"

"I think so. But why don't they favor putting more radiation into our environment?"

"You know perfectly well, Jim. Because mutations can be harmful. They cause cancer and sterility and the like."

"Precisely. So far as we've observed, there have been no beneficial mutations—which only stands to reason since mutations are chance occurrences, and the law of entropy tells us that chance processes tend toward greater disorder, not greater order. Essentially, what I'm saying is that mutation isn't sufficient as a mechanism to drive evolution."

"I can see why you might think that."

"But don't take it from me. Take it from an evolutionist—one of the staunchest evolutionists in history, in fact." Jim pulled a book off the shelf and flipped to a marked page. "Here's what Sir Julian Huxley had to say about the odds that mutations could contribute to evolution:

> "'A proportion of favorable mutations of one in a thousand does not sound much, but is probably generous. . . . And a total of a million mutational steps sounds a great deal but is probably an understatement. . . . However, let us take these figures as being reasonable estimates. With this pro-

portion, but without any selection, we should clearly have to breed a million strains (a thousand squared) to get one containing two favorable mutations; and so on, up to a thousand to the millionth power to get one containing a million. Of course this could not really happen, but it is a useful way of visualizing the fantastic odds against getting a number of favorable mutations in one strain through pure chance alone. A thousand to the millionth power, when written out, becomes a figure 1 with three million noughts [zeros] after it; and that would take three large volumes of about 500 pages each, just to print!. . . . No one would bet on anything so improbable happening.'"[16]

"Sounds to me like Huxley should have abandoned the whole idea of evolution," Dave said. "He obviously can't have thought mutation alone could do it."

"That's why he insisted that natural selection made the difference."

"But natural selection's really an empty idea."

"You and I know that, and the lawyer Norman Macbeth, author of *Darwin Retried*, argued that extensively. But Huxley might not have recognized it."

"So evolution might not really be so scientific after all. And Christianity, even with creationism, might not be so unscientific."

"Not only is Christianity not unscientific, Dave, but I believe—and so do lots of philosophers of science and historians of science—that modern science couldn't even have arisen without Christianity."

"You're kidding. Why?"

"Because Christianity provided to Western civilization an understanding of reality that could give rise to scientific ways of thinking. Other religions—like Hinduism and

Buddhism, and the Greek and Babylonian and Roman myth religions—couldn't."

"How come?"

"Did you ever study other religions very much?"

"A little bit. I read a book on comparative religions once."

"How do Hinduism and Buddhism view the material world?"

"They say it's all illusion and deception. Life's goal is to overcome the illusion so that you realize you're just part of the universal all, the one god that is everything."

"And if you thought of matter and energy as nothing but illusion, would you be likely to develop the disciplines of hypothesis, prediction, experimentation, and observation that are crucial to scientific endeavor?"

"No, I guess not."

"And suppose you were an animist, who believed everything in nature was inhabited by demonic spirits that got a charge out of tricking people. What then?"

"I suppose science wouldn't likely grow out of that either."

"And the Egyptian, Babylonian, Greek, and Roman mythologies always had their gods fighting with each other, interfering in the working of the world, right? So things weren't very predictable in that view either, were they?"

"No, they weren't."

"You see, Dave, the Bible tells us that a rational God created a universe that is ordered and predictable. Judaism believes that, and Christianity and Islam as well. But the other great world religions don't. That's why science arose in cultures that were most shaped by the Bible—particularly by Christianity, which spread more than either Judaism or Islam and has been more consistently faithful to this Biblical view of reality."[17]

"Why is that? How have Judaism and Islam diverged from it?"

"Well, in Judaism a whole new tradition arose called the cabala, a mystical and occult way of viewing reality that led to magicalism. In fact, the old alchemy movement—which thought there must be some magical way of transforming common metals into gold and silver—arose partly out of cabala. A few Christians got into that philosophy during the Middle Ages, but not many, and generally Christians strongly opposed it. And magicalism became prevalent in Islam, too, because of belief in genies. At any rate, the magical view of reality stood in the way of Islam's and post-Biblical Judaism's giving birth to science in the way Christianity did."

"Okay, Jim, I can see there are plausible reasons to reject evolution. But if it's true, then that seems to me to be an insuperable obstacle to believing the Bible."

"Let me suggest another way of thinking about this, Dave. The key question I'm putting before you is how you're going to respond to Jesus Christ, not what you think about evolution and creation. Although most Christians believe the Bible contradicts evolution—and I'm among them—I have to admit there are respectable Christian scholars who think the two can be reconciled."

"How?"

"They think the parts of the Bible that tell about creation—especially the first chapters of Genesis—are poetic and are meant to convey theological and moral principles, not to tell historical events."

"You mean sort of like the parables of Jesus?"

"Right. That's what they think. For them, it's possible to believe both the Bible and evolution. Some call themselves progressive creationists. They believe God created different kinds of life at different times through geologic history. Others call themselves theistic evolutionists. They believe God guided the evolutionary process."

"What do you think of those ideas, Jim?"

"Well, I disagree with them, both because I really think science doesn't support evolution well at all, and because I think they're misunderstanding Genesis. But if you ask me, I think their views are a whole lot more reasonable than plain old evolution. At least they can point to God as the explanation, the cause, behind the changes evolutionists say occurred."

"Yes, that would solve the problems of entropy and the high improbability of mutations causing upward development. I can see that."

"At any rate, Dave, my point is that although I'd disagree with you about evolution if you still believed in it, I don't think that has to stand in the way of your believing the Bible and accepting Jesus Christ. Other sincere, learned Christians do both, and that's one option you might consider."

"I'll think about that."

"Okay, Dave. And I'll be glad to lend you any books I have that you might find helpful."

"Thanks."

"So what's next? Got any other problems with Christianity?"

"Well, yes, as a matter of fact. With the Bible and history. I remember taking a course in ancient history in which the teacher kept claiming the Bible had its facts all wrong."

"So much the worse for the teacher, Dave."

"I suppose you're going to argue that it's historically accurate?"

"Well, we've already talked about that for the New Testament, remember?"

"Yes, but she was talking mostly about the Old Testament."

"Okay, let's focus on that. In the past century, archaeology has confirmed hundreds of specific statements in the Old Testament that historians previously had doubted because they knew of no corroborating evidence in other historical literature. For instance, Genesis tells of the cities of Sodom and Gomorrah, but no other ancient literature known mentioned them . . . until digs at Tel Mardikh, or Ebla, in the 1970s turned up over fifteen thousand clay tablets containing the daily records of the government of Ebla, and many of them mentioned dealings with Sodom and Gomorrah.

"For centuries, anti-Biblical historians believed there never was a civilization known as the Hittites, who figure prominently in the history of Israel. But in the nineteenth century, archaeologists found many references to the Hittites throughout the ancient Near Eastern world, and parts of their civilization have now been unearthed.

"I could tell you of other examples, but let it suffice to say that while thousands of archaeological discoveries have confirmed the Bible, not a single one has ever disconfirmed it."

"How do you know that?"

"Don't take my word for it. Listen to William F. Albright, the dean of American Near Eastern archaeologists." Jim pulled a fat hardback off the shelf and looked through the index quickly.

"What book is that, Jim?"

"*Understanding the Times*, by David Noebel. An incredible book, Dave. It presents, in parallel chapters, the Marxist/Leninist, Secular Humanist, and Biblical Christian worldviews and their implications in each of ten different major academic subjects—theology, philosophy, ethics, biology, psychology, sociology, law, politics, economics, and history—and then shows why the Christian worldview is to be preferred both for its truth and for its practical implications in those fields."

"Sounds fascinating. Don't suppose I could borrow that, too, could I?"

"Sure. I think you'll like it. It's filled with quotes from the top thinkers in each of the different camps, so it presents the different positions accurately."

"Sounds good. Okay, so what did this archaeologist say?"

"Here it is. He's quoted on p. 771.

"'. . . the excessive skepticism shown toward the Bible by important historical schools of the eighteenth and nineteenth centuries, certain phases of which still appear periodically, has been progressively discredited. Discovery after discovery has established the accuracy of innumerable details, and has brought increased recognition to the value of the Bible as a source of history.'"[18]

"But, Jim, listen . . . the Bible's a pretty old book, and as you say, it was written by a lot of different people in a lot of different languages—"

"Three languages, actually."

"Okay, three languages. But now it's been copied and translated and everything for thousands of years. How do we know what we have in front of us is what was originally written? Couldn't it have been changed through the years—even corrected so that errors that were in it in the first place were taken out, making it *seem* like it was really accurate when in fact originally it wasn't?"

"Here again, Dave, the Bible is unique among ancient literature. While most ancient literature is attested by only a few ancient copies—usually separated from the originals by many centuries—there are thousands of ancient manuscripts and parts of manuscripts of the various parts of the Bible extant today, and many of them, in the case of the New

Testament anyway, date from within a few decades of original composition."

"But when I was reading in Romans last night, Jim, I noticed a footnote in my Bible saying something like 'Some manuscripts read such-and-such,' something different from what I had just read. I got to looking for notes like that, and I found quite a few. How do we know what the original manuscripts really said?"

"Well, there are many variations in reading, but the vast majority affect only spellings of words or insignificant word order. Only a few affect the meaning of a passage significantly, and none of the affected passages is essential to any part of Christian teaching."

"And you say that other ancient literature isn't so well attested?"

"Right." Jim got up and found Norman Geisler and William Nix's *General Introduction to the Bible* on his shelves, then paged through it until he found what he was looking for.

"Look here, Dave. Here's a comparison between the textual evidence for the Bible and the textual evidence for other ancient literature that most historians and literary scholars accept as authentic. Caesar's *Gallic Wars* . . . we have only ten ancient manuscripts, the oldest dating from a thousand years after Caesar wrote. About twenty-two hundred years separate the oldest manuscript of Homer's *Odyssey* from the poet himself. Homer's *Iliad* has more existing ancient manuscripts—643—than any other ancient literature except the New Testament, which has almost nine times as many. Only forty lines—a fifth of a percent—of the New Testament have textual variations that put their meaning in serious doubt, while 764 lines—about 5 percent—of the *Iliad* and 10 percent of the *Mahabharata*—the sacred book of the Hindus—are in doubt. No other ancient literature even begins to compare with the New Testament for textual authenticity."[19]

"What about the Old Testament, though?"

"Well, a different fact gives us great confidence in the authenticity of the Old Testament. Because the Jews believed it was God's Word, they took amazing care when copying it. They weren't permitted to copy whole sentences, clauses, phrases, or even words at a time; they had to read a letter from the master and write it into the copy; read another letter and write it; read another and write it; and so on."

"Good grief! That's pretty painstaking. It must have taken them forever to produce a whole copy of any book of the Old Testament."

"It was slow, all right, but it was also highly accurate. If they made a mistake, they had to mark the sheet, throw it away, and start a fresh one to be sure no one mistakenly thought the flawed sheet was correct. In fact, it's precisely because they were so careful with the texts that we don't have so many manuscripts of the Old Testament; flawed ones were destroyed.

"The scribes also had some ingenious methods of checking for accuracy. They counted the number of words in the Old Testament, and in each of its books and, when a copy was finished, did random checks throughout, knowing what word should come at precisely the middle and at other spots throughout it. No other ancient writing got such great care in copying as the Old Testament, and again, no serious variation in the text affects any essential Biblical teaching."[20]

"Jim, until we started talking, I would never have imagined there was so much evidence for Christian faith. You've really surprised me."

"So what's your decision?"

"I'm not deciding yet, Jim. I'm thinking, and I have to admit I'm pretty close to believing in Jesus."

"Good. I'm praying for that."

"I figured you were. Of course, I don't know what to make of that either, because I don't know if I believe in prayer."

"One thing at a time, Dave."

"Yeah. Well, there are still some other problems I'd like to discuss, if you don't mind. I suppose you might be getting tired of my questions by now, wondering if they're just excuses—"

"No, Dave. You're honest about them. I've met some other people who weren't—people who keep going back to the same problems over and over again even though I've shown them solid answers and they can't give me any rebuttals. Eventually I realize I'm wasting my time. But I've noticed that you think carefully about what I say, and when you're convinced—or at least have seen enough to ease your objections—you move on to something new. I respect that."

"Good. Well, I do have other problems—like, for instance, if Jesus Christ was so wonderful and taught His people to love, how come so many terrible things have been done in the past by Christianity?"

"Not just in the past, Dave, but—I'm sad to say—even today. Good question, but it's nearly midnight and I've got to be at work in the morning. Come on over tomorrow night and we'll talk again."

"Sure, Jim."

Chapter 9

Time for Some Decisions

The next evening, Dave seemed different somehow. Not resigned, really, but like somebody who's struggled a long time with something and has nearly resolved it.

"Jim," he said, "I really like what I've learned about Jesus. And you—well, you're my best friend. But some of the things Christians have done are pretty bad. Like the Crusades, or how colonial empires treated people. Doesn't Christianity bear the blame for those things?"

"You've got a legitimate point there, Dave. But first, let's make a distinction."

"Between what?"

"Between Christianity as a faith and Christianity as the collection of all the people who have professed that faith, whether sincerely or insincerely."

"Sounds reasonable."

"I've been talking to you about the Christian faith, and particularly about Jesus Himself and your need to have a relationship with Him, to trust Him for the forgiveness of your sins and obey Him as your Lord."

"Right."

"Your beef really isn't with Jesus, is it? I mean, you've read the Gospels. Did you see anything about Jesus in them that you didn't like?"

"No, I guess not."

"Anything evil or foolish about Him?"

"No."

"And you've seen a lot of good reasons to believe the Christian faith, right?"

"Yes. I wouldn't say I've seen 100 percent proof yet, but I realize the problem with demanding that."

"Okay, so your problem is not with Christianity as a faith, but with some people who claim to be—and in some cases really are—Christians, right?"

"Right."

"Okay. Well, Christianity's record isn't perfect. Christians have made many mistakes, sometimes doing things they knew full well were wrong."

"Just as you and I do, right?"

"Right. After all, Jesus did say He came to save sinners, not the 'righteous.' So it shouldn't be surprising if we find a bunch of sinners in church. It's supposed to be a haven for sinners who have been forgiven."

"Right."

"The Bible says no one will be without sin in this life. So in churches, sinners gather to rejoice that they're forgiven and to encourage each other to serve Christ better. Since the Christian Church was designed as a hospital for the spiritually sick, it shouldn't surprise us if we find spiritually sick people in it, right?"

"Sure. That makes sense."

"And besides, the truth of the message doesn't stand or fall with the perfection of those who believe it. It is to Jesus

Christ's claim on your life that you need to answer, not to Christians."

"Still, what about the terrible things that have been done in the name of religion?"

"Many of them were real and inexcusable. I won't pretend they weren't. But some of them weren't really done by Christians at all—just by power-hungry people who masqueraded as Christians to get Christian people to trust them and support what they were doing. Much of the impetus toward the Crusades, for instance, came not from the Christian Church but from kings and princes eager to expand their realms and capture the riches of the East. And colonialism was a program not of churches but of political empires. The two got entangled from time to time, but they were distinct in principle."

"But the Crusades and colonialism were so cruel and caused so much suffering!"

"Yes and no. We really need to be careful to be fair in our judgments of history. A couple of things can blur those judgments."

"Such as?"

"For one thing, we can apply modern standards to times and cultures that hadn't yet become aware of them."

"You mean we shouldn't apply the same standards to everyone everywhere? What's wrong in one culture, or in one time, might be right in another?"

"No, not exactly. What's wrong is wrong, no matter where or when. God's standards of justice and righteousness don't change."

"Then what are you getting at?"

"Well, while the standards of right and wrong don't change, the standards of culpability might, depending on how much people understand. You read the Gospel of John recently, didn't you?"

"Yes."

"Do you remember reading the story of Jesus healing a man who had been born blind?"

"Yes."

"Remember how the Pharisees responded?"

"They kept trying to insist that Jesus couldn't have healed him. But the healed man worshiped Jesus."

"Well, Jesus was pretty harsh with the Pharisees because they refused to believe He'd healed the man, wasn't He?"

"I guess so. I don't remember for sure."

"Look at it here at the end of John 9 . . ." Jim handed his Bible to Dave. "One Pharisee asked if Jesus was saying they were blind. What did Jesus say?"

"'If you were blind, you would have no sin; but now you say, "We see." Therefore your sin remains.' I think I see what you're driving at."

"What is it?"

"Well, the Pharisees claimed to be such wise men, but they didn't recognize Jesus for who He was, and they kept insisting the blind man hadn't been healed—when obviously he had been. They claimed to know a lot, but they really didn't, so they deserved harsh judgment because they claimed they knew so much."

"Right. You see, they'd have been wrong to have opposed Jesus anyway, but their error was compounded because they claimed to be so knowledgeable. If they'd really been so knowledgeable, they'd have recognized Jesus as the Messiah."

"Okay. But how does this relate to the terrible things done by Christians in the past?"

"As I was saying, the standards of right and wrong don't change, but standards of blame can be suited to the situation and the people involved. Many of the things we recognize immediately today as wrong weren't easily recognized as wrong at certain times in history. There were long periods when people hadn't realized the consequences of some things, or hadn't realized that their actions were inconsistent with certain principles they held."

"Give me an example."

"One example is the close connection between church and state. Early Christianity grew up in a world in which the Roman Empire, which had been the chief stabilizing force in the Western world, was on the decline. Its decline left a serious power vacuum in which anarchic and tyrannous forces could easily take advantage of weaker people. But the Church was growing rapidly, becoming more influential. Church leaders, eager to counteract the chaotic tendencies of the decline of the Roman Empire, began to take on civil powers. Eventually a close alliance between ecclesiastical and civil governments arose. For a while things went pretty well, with some exceptions. It really took several centuries before the dangers inherent in the alliance became clear. Meanwhile, lots of things were done consistent with that alliance that we would recognize immediately today as wrong but that weren't so easily recognized as wrong then."

"So those things really were wrong, but those who did them might not have been so culpable as we'd think today?"

"Essentially, that's it."

"Okay, I can understand that."

"Another thing that can blur our judgments of history is focusing only on what went wrong and forgetting what went right. And that happens in two ways. First, with regard to a particular event or series of events, we see only the bad effects and not the good. Second, we tend to focus only on the bad things done in the name of Christianity and forget that there were lots of good things, too."

"So you're saying the Crusades and colonialism—besides having been conducted in part by people who really weren't Christians at all—weren't all bad?"

"That's right. While there was a lot of killing in the

Crusades, and plenty of greedy men used them as an excuse to gain riches and power, they weren't an unmixed evil. Remember, the Crusades began as a defensive action, keeping an expansionist Moslem empire from taking over all of Europe and destroying the civil liberties the people there enjoyed—liberties far beyond what most of the rest of the world had ever enjoyed, even if they weren't as great as ours today. In fact, the Crusades delivered lots of people from tyranny and superstition that had held them in political and intellectual bondage for generations."

"What about colonialism? Wasn't it really oppressive?"

"I won't defend the intentions of many of the colonial rulers. They were after power and gold for their national treasuries. Nonetheless, economic history indicates that their hopes were largely frustrated. As a matter of fact, acquiring and maintaining colonies usually cost the colonial powers far more than they gained from them. Colonization actually did more good than harm even to the colonies themselves, since it resulted in the rapid modernization of the economies of many lands that would have continued to suffer deep poverty otherwise."

"You know, Jim, I should have thought of that. I remember in a course on economic development I took a few years ago being required to read something by Lord P. T. Bauer, a British economist, in which he showed that parts of the world that were colonized actually developed much faster than other parts. In fact, he demonstrated a strong correlation between prior colonization and higher levels of economic development and higher standards of living in Third World countries today, and even showed that net transfers of wealth tended to go from mother countries to colonies, not the reverse."[21]

"That's interesting. I've never heard of Bauer. But what he says fits right in with what Adam Smith, founder of modern economics, argued two centuries ago in *The Wealth of Nations*.

He showed clearly, from Britain's own accounts, that the colonies cost the United Kingdom far more than she ever got from them."[22]

"So the bad side of colonialism was that it often involved political oppression. But the good side was that it usually brought more rapid economic development than would have happened otherwise. I can see that," Dave said.

"And even on a civil liberties scale, colonialism—although it fell short of contemporary Western standards—was usually preferable to the local alternatives at the time. Colonies rarely were formed in territories governed by enlightened governments. Usually they replaced anarchy or tribal warfare. In fact, the African continent never knew so many years of peace and general prosperity as it did under colonial rule. And since the colonies were 'freed,' most of Africa has suffered almost non-stop tribal warfare."

"Yes, I see what you mean."

"Anyway, we have to avoid looking only at the dark side of particular things. We should also be sure to give proper credit where it's due."

"And what does Christianity deserve credit for in history?"

"The Christian Church has been the primary stimulus to lots of good things in human history. Most of the great colleges and universities in the Western world began as Christian colleges—even seminaries, like Harvard and Yale and Princeton and Dartmouth. Thousands of hospitals around the world began as missionary clinics. Hundreds of languages around the world were never reduced to writing until Christian missionaries, with Wycliffe Bible Translators and other organizations, went and learned the languages, devised alphabets and writing for them, and began to put literature into them—especially the Bible, but other things too, eventually."

"And you've already pointed out that science owes its origin to Christianity," Dave said.

"Yes, and so does our modern, productive economy."[23]

"Oh? I'd never heard that before."

"Yes. Partly it's a matter of worldview again. If you believe the world is illusion and that your highest goal is to escape the illusion by denying all desire—"

"You're not likely to develop much of an economy. And the same if you have a magical view of the world—you can't depend on anything to be predictable, so you can't plan and save and invest, and thus the economy doesn't grow. No wonder places like Asia and Africa have been so long in catching up with the West economically."

"Exactly, Dave. In fact, statistical studies show that, in general, the poorest nations are least influenced by Christianity and most dominated by animism, spiritism, Hinduism, and Buddhism—the worldviews farthest from Christianity."

"But what about Japan and Taiwan and the other Asian countries whose economies have been growing so fast lately?"

"Actually, Dave, although there aren't many Christians in Japan, Christian business and political principles have had a very strong role in shaping the economic systems and business culture of Japan. In the late nineteenth century, Japan actually sent a delegation of government and business leaders around the West to find out what made the West so productive.[24] They saw things like division of labor and assembly lines and capital formation and realized they were important. But they saw that even more important were Christian cultural and ethical principles like saving, service to customers, market freedom, and so on."

"*Christian* ethical principles?"

"Yes, many of those principles are rooted in the Bible, and many of them were first developed by Roman Catholic scholastic thinkers, like Thomas Aquinas and the Salamanca school in Spain, and by the Reformers, like John Calvin. In fact, Adam Smith, who was actually a professor of moral philosophy and was trained for the Presbyterian ministry, studied some of their works—and the works of people who followed in their footsteps—and his understanding of economics was in many ways an application of their ethical principles to market relationships."[25]

"Fascinating. I never heard that before."

"At any rate, Japan's economic boom early in the twentieth century came about largely because Japan copied the ethical, cultural, and organizational patterns of the West, which were rooted in Christian thinking. And after World War II, Japan's constitution was written by General Douglas MacArthur, a Christian who purposely wove those principles into the constitution."

"So Japan's wealth is rooted in Christian culture, even though not many Japanese are Christians?"

"Right. And Taiwan's boom after the Communist revolution in Mainland China has similar origins. In fact, many leaders of Taiwan's government were Christians, and that nation's chief finance minister was a Christian who carefully wove Christian principles into the development of Taiwan's economic policy."[26]

"And places like Korea and Singapore have followed suit?"

"Yes. And of course, Singapore and Hong Kong had the advantage of being British colonies, so they picked up the cultural, political, ethical, and organizational principles from Britain."

"So Christianity has really had a lot to do with causing economic development all over the world, hasn't it?"

"Yes, Dave. And there are other good things Christianity has done through the centuries. But these are all outward things. What's even more important is what Christianity has done for the human spirit."

"And what's that?"

"Although Christianity wisely warns against any expectations of human-induced utopia,[27] it does offer the world hope through the promise that God is working things out, that He sent Jesus to pay for our sins, that Jesus overcame our greatest enemy—death—and that we can be assured of forgiveness and eternal friendship with God by faith in Jesus."

"You know, Jim, come to think of it, that's a pretty different outlook on life from what I see in the philosophers, particularly when it comes to death. They don't offer anybody any hope. Aeschylus, for instance, denied that there's any life after death, and Theocritus said something like, 'There is hope only for those who are alive, but those who have died are without hope.'"

"Yes, and the Roman poet Catullus said, 'When once our brief light sets, there is one perpetual night through which we must sleep.'"

"Pretty depressing," Dave said.

"But Jesus said, in John 11:25-26, 'I am the resurrection and the life. He who believes in Me, though he may die, he shall live. And whoever lives and believes in Me shall never die.'"

"Yes. I remember reading that. He said that to the girl whose brother Lazarus had died, didn't He?"

"Right. And then He raised Lazarus from the dead. Jesus promises eternal life to all who trust Him as Savior and submit to Him as Lord. He also promises a wonderful life on earth for those who commit themselves to Him. In John 10:10 He said, 'I have come that they may have life, and that they may have it more abundantly.'"

"Boy, what a difference! In fact, just last night I was reading in one of Paul's letters to Timothy, and he had an amazing attitude toward his own death, which I guess he expected to come soon."

"Yes. What was it he wrote?"

Dave picked up Jim's Bible and found the verses. "'. . . the time of my departure is at hand. I have fought the good fight, I have finished the race, I have kept the faith. Finally, there is laid up for me the crown of righteousness, which the Lord, the righteous Judge, will give to me on that Day; and not to me only, but also to all who have loved His appearing.' That doesn't sound much like Jean-Paul Sartre, does it? He concluded in his philosophy that suicide was the only sensible choice for anyone who really understood this world."

"You've got it, Dave. The problem of death is real, but in Jesus Christ and His resurrection it is solved. That's why Paul wrote, in 1 Corinthians 15:51-57, 'Behold, I tell you a mystery: We shall not all sleep, but we shall all be changed—in a moment, in the twinkling of an eye, at the last trumpet. For the trumpet will sound, and the dead will be raised incorruptible, and we shall be changed. For this corruptible must put on incorruption, and this mortal must put on immortality. So when this corruptible has put on incorruption, and this mortal has put on immortality, then shall be brought to pass the saying that is written: "Death is swallowed up in victory." "O Death, where is your sting? O Hades, where is your victory?" The sting of death is sin, and the strength of sin is the law. But thanks be to God, who gives us the victory through our Lord Jesus Christ.'

"And then Paul concludes by showing the connection between that hopeful view of our future after death and a different way of living today: 'Therefore, my beloved brethren, be steadfast, immovable, always abounding in the work of the Lord, knowing that your labor is not in vain in the Lord.'"

"Okay, Jim. I'm with you more and more. But tell me,

does the Bible offer the world any hope of escaping the threat of war?"

"Well, the Bible is realistic. After all, that's where we learn just how sinful man is. So long as men remain sinners, there will probably always be war, or the threat of war. But Christianity does encourage people to learn to understand each other, to forgive each other for wrongs suffered—"

"Yes, like when Jesus said to turn the other cheek and to bless those who persecute you."

"Right. And the Bible tells people to love each other, to protect the innocent against aggressors who would harm them. And Christianity tells us that ultimately God will intervene in the affairs of men and bring war to an end—although we don't know just when or how.

"Ultimately, Dave, it comes down to individuals. Real change for the world begins with change in our own hearts. Jesus promises to make that change in anyone who gives his life to Him. Will you do that, Dave? Right now?"

"Look, Jim, over these last few months you've given me some really persuasive reasons to become a Christian. I won't pretend you haven't. I want to believe. But if I do, I know I'm going to have to change some things about how I live. Like living with my girlfriend."

"Dave, everyone desires to rule his own life. But that's not how God intended things to be. God made us to love and obey Him, and He says that's the only way for us really to be successful and happy in life. If we try to run our own lives instead, we just mess things up—like when you got those girls pregnant and then pushed them into getting abortions."

"Yes, I see what you mean. I do seem to keep making a mess of things, don't I?"

"Sure, you do. That's because, as Paul puts it in Romans 6, since you aren't a Christian, you're a slave to sin. You *think* you're ruling your life, but actually sin is ruling you. If you really want to be set free, you've got to give control of your life over to Jesus. In Galatians 5, Paul says that self-control is a fruit of the Holy Spirit, part of what God builds in us when we yield to Him. If you want self-control, Dave, you're going to have to give up self-rule."

"But I'd have to give up an awful lot of stuff to be a Christian, Jim."

"Like what?"

"I like wine and beer and going to parties, for one thing."

"Well, the Bible doesn't say you can't drink or go to parties. It says you aren't supposed to get drunk, but Psalm 104 actually says that God made grapes to give us wine for our enjoyment."

"And Jesus made wine at a wedding party, didn't He?"

"Sure. Now, there are parties, and there are parties. Parties where everybody gets soused and people are sleeping around—"

"I don't even like those anymore."

"Of course not. They seem fun at first, but pretty soon you see how empty they are, and how empty the people who go to them all the time are."

"That's for sure."

"Look, what you need to be willing to give up as a Christian is simply sin. And if you really think about it, no sin is any fun for long, is it?"

"You're right."

"So you give up things like lying, cheating, stealing, being unfaithful to people, being discontent and coveting what belongs to others."

"What about living with my girlfriend?"

"The Bible says that's sin, Dave, unless you're married. You'd have to be willing to stop that if you wanted Jesus to rule your life."

"That's pretty tough."

"It's a choice you have to make. Look what living with girls outside marriage did to them and to their babies."

"Not much good, I guess."

"So either marry Sarah, so you can give her the lifelong commitment she deserves from someone who's going to live with her, or move out and stop taking advantage of her."

"I guess there's no getting around it."

"Not if you're going to be honest with Sarah, honest with yourself, and—most of all—honest with Jesus."

"I don't know, Jim."

"Well, Dave, you do have to give up some things if you're going to be a Christian. But look what you get in return: forgiveness, eternal life, the promise of God that as you learn to live His way your life will become rich and full. Most of all, you get God Himself, who's worth more than anything in the world."

"Jim, I want it. I want it, but it's like I'm stuck."

"Dave, Jesus said, 'If anyone desires to come after Me, let him deny himself, and take up his cross, and follow Me.' You know something, Dave?"

"What?"

"If you're honest with yourself, you'll know it's really not Sarah or anything else you don't want to give up for Jesus' sake. It's yourself. You're intent on being Number One in your life. And frankly, from what you've told me about what you've done, choosing yourself over Jesus is pretty dumb."

"You're not exactly diplomatic, are you, Jim?"

"You mean, when I care about somebody, I don't fool around with telling him lies to make him feel good?"

Dave hesitated a minute.

"Look, Dave, Jesus says you have to deny yourself and follow Him. But listen to what He says after that: 'For whoever desires to save his life will lose it, but whoever loses his life for My sake will find it. For what profit is it to a man if he gains the whole world, and loses his own soul? Or what will a man give in exchange for his soul?' There's nothing to gain in being true to yourself if your self is a cad, Dave. But Jesus says if you lose your life for His sake, you'll find it."

"And I'll be able to forgive myself for what I did to Anna and Marcy?"

"Yes, Dave. Or, more to the point, you'll know that God has forgiven you and cleansed you, and that's what really counts."

Again Dave was silent for a while.

Jim continued, "Dave, Jesus promises great blessing to those who follow Him. Whatever we leave behind, we get far more in return. You might have to leave Sarah. She's almost a wife to you, but if you're not willing to marry her—"

"Or if she's not willing to marry me!"

"Either way. If you don't get married, you're going to have to live apart and stop sleeping together. But Jesus said, in Mark 10:29-30, '... there is no one who has left house or brothers or sisters or father or mother or wife or children or lands, for My sake and the gospel's, who shall not receive a hundredfold now in this time—houses and brothers and sisters and mothers and children and lands, with persecutions—and in the age to come, eternal life.'

"You see, Dave, when you become a Christian, you become a member of a great family that stretches all around the world. Other Christians are delighted to meet you. When you need a place to stay, you're welcome in the homes of Christians. When you need friends or family, Christians stand ready to be friends and family to you. When you can't provide for your own food or clothing, Christians will provide for you. Indeed, Christians are told by Jesus to do these things for others, too, but especially for Christians.

"Jesus was realistic about the Christian life. There will be troubles and hardships; we will have to give up some things we've liked. But what we receive in exchange is worth infinitely more."

"Can't it wait, Jim?"

"I can't force you, Dave. But remember the parable Jesus told about the rich man whose fields produced too much for his barns?"

"Yes. He built more barns for his harvests and said, 'Eat, drink, and be merry,' but that night God came and took his life."

"And God called him a fool for having chosen this world's goods over God. And he was also a fool for not having considered the possibility that he was going to die and for not having prepared himself for it. That's a possibility for you, too, Dave. How do you know you won't get in a fatal accident on your way home tonight? What will your life be worth then?"

"But won't I get another chance? Maybe through reincarnation?"

"What you need is not more lives in which to mess things up. You need a new kind of life entirely, one that you can only get from Christ. And besides, the Bible says there are no second chances. Hebrews 9:27 says we die once, and then we meet God's judgment. What we do in this life is what counts, Dave."

"But maybe I can change my life on my own."

"Does your past experience give you much hope of that?"

"No, I guess not."

"Dave, Jesus likens people to trees—good trees and bad trees. He says the good trees bear good fruit, but the bad trees bear bad fruit. Of ourselves, we can't produce good fruit. We can only produce bad fruit."

"So how do we become good trees?"

"We have to be changed—changed by Someone other than ourselves. That's why Paul said in 2 Corinthians 5:17-18 that anyone who becomes a Christian becomes a new creature—old things pass away, new things come—because God is reconciled to him through Christ. You don't need another chance, Dave. You need a new heart. Only Jesus can give you that."

"Can He really forgive me for what I've done?"

"Remember King David and Psalm 51?"

"Yes."

"You can take hope from Paul, too. He wrote in 1 Timothy 1 that even though he had been a blasphemer and a persecutor of Christians, God had shown him mercy, forgiving him for Jesus' sake. And then he added, 'This is a faithful saying and worthy of all acceptance, that Christ Jesus came into the world to save sinners, of whom I am chief.'"

"I remember reading that. I really wanted to be able to say that, too."

"If God could forgive David and Paul, He can forgive you."

"But how can He do that?"

"Because the precious blood of Jesus paid all the debt your sins had built up. Believe in Him, and His punishment will be credited to your account; His righteousness will be given to you, too."

"He would really accept me, just the way I am?"

"Yes, Dave. Jesus said in John 6:37, '. . . the one who comes to Me I will by no means cast out.' And John, in 1 John 1:9, wrote, 'If we confess our sins, He is faithful and just to forgive us our sins and to cleanse us from all unrighteousness.'"

"I want to believe, Jim. I want to believe. But I don't have enough faith."

"It's not a matter of how *much* faith you have, Dave. It's a matter of whether you have any at all. You didn't have absolute faith this building wouldn't collapse when you walked into it, did you? But you came in anyway, and it was the strength of the building, not the quality of your faith, that kept the building up.

"You don't need to have absolute faith to become a Christian. Just faith enough to admit you're a sinner and to ask Jesus to forgive you and take control of your life."

"But what if I become a Christian and then my friends all ridicule me—and believe me, they will. They'd think I was faking it, because they know how strongly I've argued against Christianity for years."

"Well, would you rather have them ridicule you, or have God say to you, 'You fool, this night I will require your soul of you'? Do you want honor from men or from God?"

"But what if I turn my back on Christ later?"

"It's possible you will, Dave—although I doubt it. You're a pretty strong character. Once you've made up your mind, you don't cave in easily. But even if you do, He'll never give up on you, and He'll pull you back to Him. Jesus promised, in Matthew 28:20, to always be with those who trust Him. He can strengthen you so you *won't* turn your back on Him, just as He strengthened Stephen when he was stoned, and Paul when he preached all over the Roman Empire and finally died a martyr's death, and all the other apostles."

"But, Jim, maybe you don't really know me that well. I can be a real coward sometimes. Especially when my friends are really pressuring me to do something."

"Then you can draw courage from the Lord, Dave. And I believe you'll find it easier than you think, because you'll have begun to know the joy of living with Christ. Thousands of Christians were martyred during the first few centuries after Jesus' death. They had all experienced such joy in Jesus that they never complained about their persecution and death. They went joyfully to be burned alive or torn apart by lions or crucified as Jesus had been—often singing praises to Jesus on the way. They were such strong witnesses that thousands who saw them martyred became Christians as a result. God can do the same in you."

"How about if I put off receiving Christ until the end of my life? Then at least I'd know I wouldn't deny Him later."

"Of course, you can't be sure you'll know when you're about to die. Suppose your death is sudden, in an accident. Or suppose you're in surgery someday and lapse into a coma and never wake up, even though you live for years afterward?

"Dave, God promises to give anyone who trusts in Jesus strength enough to stay faithful to Him. That's why Paul wrote, in Philippians 1:6 that he was 'confident of this very thing, that He who has begun a good work in you will complete it until the day of Jesus Christ.' You see, Dave, when you become a Christian, you're *His* workmanship, not your own, and He doesn't leave jobs half finished."

Both men were silent for a while. At last Jim said, "Dave, here . . . Take my Bible. Open it to Romans 8 and start reading at verse 28."

Dave took it and read, "'And we know that all things work together for good to those who love God, to those who are the called according to His purpose.'"

"Do you love God, Dave? Think of what He's done, of who He is. Do you love Him?"

"Yes, Jim, I think I do."

"Go ahead. Keep on reading."

"'For whom He foreknew, He also predestined to be conformed to the image of His Son, that He might be the firstborn among many brethren. Moreover whom He predestined, these He also called; whom He called, these He also justified; and whom He justified, these He also glorified.'"

"Notice something, Dave? Everyone who starts, finishes. Everyone who ever becomes a Christian in the first place eventually gets glorified."

"Yes, I see that."

"Now read what comes next."

"'What then shall we say to these things? If God is for us,

who can be against us? He who did not spare His own Son, but delivered Him up for us all, how shall He not with Him also freely give us all things? Who shall bring a charge against God's elect? It is God who justifies. Who is he who condemns? It is Christ who died, and furthermore is also risen, who is even at the right hand of God, who also makes intercession for us.'"

"You see, Dave, when you become a Christian, *God* is on your side! Then nothing can defeat you. God's the One who really has a right to charge us with sin, but He doesn't; He justifies us. Christ has the right to condemn us, but instead He prays for us. Now go ahead."

"'Who shall separate us from the love of Christ?' I remember reading this a few days ago. It's beautiful. And I wished then that I could believe it."

"So, read it again."

"'Who shall separate us from the love of Christ? Shall tribulation, or distress, or persecution, or famine, or nakedness, or peril, or sword? As it is written: "For Your sake we are killed all day long; we are accounted as sheep for the slaughter." Yet in all these things we are more than conquerors through Him who loved us. For I am persuaded that neither death nor life, nor angels nor principalities nor powers, nor things present nor things to come, nor height nor depth, nor any other created thing, shall be able to separate us from the love of God which is in Christ Jesus our Lord.'"

"Dave, you don't have to fear whether you'll stay true to Christ. God Himself will keep you true to Him."

"That's what I want, Jim. I really do. I want that kind of relationship with God. How do I get it?"

"You confess to God that you're a sinner, ask Him to forgive you, and trust Jesus as your Savior and submit to Him as your Master."

"But how?"

"If you want me to, I can suggest something you might say to God in prayer."

"Please do."

"Okay. If you'll pray this, and if you mean it from your heart, you can be assured that Christ will come into your life as your Savior and Lord.

"Lord Jesus, I acknowledge that You are my Creator, that together with the Father and the Holy Spirit, You created the universe. I agree that for this reason I owe You absolute obedience, love, and honor. But, Jesus, I have dishonored You. I have sinned in many ways, doing what I shouldn't have done and not doing what I should. Because of my sins, I fall far short of Your glory and deserve Your judgment. Jesus, I'm sorry. Please forgive me. I want to be changed, Lord. I can't change myself, but I'm willing for You to change me, and I give You my life for that purpose. Forgive me, give me Your righteousness, and reconcile me to God the Father. I know the life You've called me to is difficult, and I could never live it on my own. But I trust You to work in me, to change me to become more like You. I thank You that other Christians can encourage and help me. Thank You for dying to pay the penalty for my sins on the cross, and for rising from the dead in victory over sin and death. And thank You for giving me that victory. Amen."

Chapter 10

Growing in Christ

Perhaps Dave's story is your own. Some Christian has told you about Jesus, and at last you've given your life to Him. Now you need to learn how to live and grow as a Christian. Or perhaps Jim's story is yours. You've told someone about Christ, he's become a Christian, and now you need to help him move on in the Christian life. Whether you're a new Christian yourself, or helping a new Christian to grow, you need to know about Christian growth.

When you were born again, your sins were taken away from you and you were made clean in Christ. Remember, this didn't happen because you've done anything to earn it—it is a gift from God.

> Therefore, having been justified by faith, we have peace with God through our Lord Jesus Christ, through whom also we have access by faith into this grace in which we stand, and rejoice in hope of the glory of God. . . . But God demonstrates His own love toward us, in that while we were still sinners, Christ died for us. Much more then, hav-

ing now been justified by His blood, we shall be saved from wrath through Him. For if when we were enemies we were reconciled to God by the death of His Son, much more, having been reconciled, we shall be saved by His life. (Romans 5:1-2, 8-10)

In a sense, when you were born again you became a baby, a spiritual child in Christ. To become mature, you need to grow. If you're in Jim's position—you've introduced someone to Christ—you need to be faithful to him and help him grow. The rest of this chapter can help you do that. If you're in Dave's position—you've recently become a Christian—you need to grow. Here are some things that can help you.

Growing Through Scripture

God calls Christians to love and serve others. That doesn't come naturally, since we're sinners. Christ gives us power to break the patterns of sin, but it takes time and effort. "Therefore, laying aside all malice, all guile, hypocrisy, envy, and all evil speaking," wrote Peter, "as newborn babes, desire the pure milk of the word, that you may grow thereby" (1 Peter 2:1-2).

The Bible is our chief and only infallible source of instruction from God about the Christian life. It is a major means God uses to sanctify us—to separate us from sinful patterns of life and make us pure and holy. Thus, Jesus prayed to the Father for His disciples, "Sanctify them by Your truth. Your word is truth" (John 17:17). One psalmist wrote, "How can a young man cleanse his way? By taking heed according to Your word. . . . Your word I have hidden in my heart, that I might not sin against You" (Psalm 119:9, 11). One excellent way to grow in Christ is to hide God's Word in our hearts—that is, to study and memorize and meditate on it, as the psalmist did.

When God was preparing Joshua to take Moses' place as leader of the Israelites, He said to him, "This Book of the Law shall not depart from your mouth, but you shall meditate in it day and night, that you may observe to do according to all that is written in it. For then you will make your way prosperous, and then you will have good success" (Joshua 1:8). This indicates that the law—chiefly the Ten Commandments—is a source of instruction from God that will, if we follow it, make us prosper in God's sight. So the Ten Commandments would be good things to include in early verses you memorize. In fact, Psalm 1 makes it clear that knowing God's law is crucial to spiritual growth:

> Blessed is the man who walks not in the counsel of the ungodly, nor stands in the path of sinners, nor sits in the seat of the scornful; but his delight is in the law of the Lord, and in His law he meditates day and night. He shall be like a tree planted by the rivers of water, that brings forth its fruit in its season, whose leaf also shall not wither; and whatever he does shall prosper. The ungodly are not so, but are like the chaff which the wind drives away. Therefore the ungodly shall not stand in the judgment, nor sinners in the congregation of the righteous. For the Lord knows the way of the righteous, but the way of the ungodly shall perish.

But there's more to the Christian life than God's law. We need to understand His grace as well, and to grow to be more and more like Jesus. Thus the Apostle Paul wrote:

> Therefore, as the elect of God, holy and beloved, put on tender mercies, kindness, humbleness of mind, meekness, longsuffering; bearing with one another, and forgiving one another, if anyone has a complaint against another; even

155

as Christ forgave you, so you do also. And above all these things put on love, which is the bond of perfection. And let the peace of God rule in your hearts, to which also you were called in one body; and be thankful. Let the word of Christ dwell in you richly in all wisdom, teaching and admonishing one another in psalms, hymns, and spiritual songs, singing with grace in your hearts to the Lord. And whatever you do in word or deed, do all in the name of the Lord Jesus, giving thanks to God the Father through Him. (Colossians 3:12-17)

For the wonderful relationships to develop among Christians as Paul describes them here, we need to be reminded continually of the things Jesus taught us, and so it would be a good idea to memorize many of the words of Jesus from the Gospels. You might start with John 10:10—"I have come that they may have life, and that they may have it more abundantly"—a wonderful promise to Christians.

Many passages in the Old and New Testaments have become especially precious to Christians through the ages— passages that remind us of God's love, of His forgiveness toward us, of Christ's victory over evil, or of the glorious future we have as sons of God. I recommend that you get the Scripture Memory Packs available from The Navigators (P.O. Box 6000, Colorado Springs, CO 80934)—packs of thirty-six cards, each with a verse on it that you can memorize; each pack includes instruction in good methods to make memorizing easier. The packs have good selections of verses especially helpful to new Christians. It's also helpful to have a partner in memorizing verses—someone who will check up on your progress and for whom you can do the same service. The partnership can make the work easier and more enjoyable.

In addition to memorizing Scripture, you want to read and meditate on it. Begin with one or two of the Gospels, where you'll get a picture of Christ Himself. Even if you read them before you became a Christian, read them again; you'll appreciate them, and Him, more now. Then read some of the New Testament epistles, which will explain much about Christian faith and life. Then go back and read about the beginning of the world in Genesis and the call of God's people in Exodus, Deuteronomy, and Joshua. The Proverbs are wonderful sources of wisdom about everyday life, as well as about your life with God. The Psalms are helpful in learning to commune with God and to appreciate His goodness. Some people read five Psalms and a chapter of Proverbs each day, thus finishing each book every month, in addition to their other Bible reading. That's a good practice, and I recommend it, but you'll need to establish a pattern that works best for you—and it will surely change from time to time throughout your Christian life.

Once you've read these things, it would be good to go back and read straight through the New Testament, paying attention especially to what you learn about Jesus, about the early Christians, and about the practices that can help you grow as a Christian. Then go back and do the same in the Old Testament. You'll find yourself especially interested in certain books of the Bible, so take time to study those carefully; when you do this, you can find books in Christian bookstores to help you understand them better.

What does it mean to meditate on the Bible? It simply means to read a portion, think carefully about it, and then mull it over in your mind again and again, growing to appreciate the rich lessons in it. The very repetition necessary to memorize verses can take you a long way toward effective meditation. You can also get help in this practice from Matthew Henry's *Directions for Daily Communion with God* (Grand Rapids, MI: Baker, 1978).

Growing Through Prayer

Another important avenue of spiritual growth is prayer—conversation with God. In prayer we tell God our thoughts, our needs, our desires; and in turn, He communicates back to us His desires about our lives, His care for us, and many things that will help us to be secure and at peace with Him and to know what He wants us to do.

A healthy prayer life grows in part out of our careful use of the Bible. "If you abide in Me, and My words abide in you, you shall ask what you desire, and it shall be done for you," Jesus said (John 15:7). The Bible instructs us about God's will through principle, command, and example. And the Apostle John tells us, "And this is the confidence that we have in Him, that if we ask anything according to His will, He hears us. And if we know that He hears us, whatever we ask, we know that we have the petitions that we have asked of Him" (1 John 5:14-15).

To every Christian, Jesus sends the Holy Spirit—the third Person of the Trinity—to be a "Comforter" (John 14:16, 25). The word "Comforter" translates a Greek word meaning "one called alongside." The Holy Spirit dwells in and with us throughout life, teaching us what we need to know from God, as we listen to Him and study His Word. ". . . when He, the Spirit of truth, has come," Jesus said, "He will guide you into all truth; for He will not speak on His own authority, but whatever He hears He will speak; and He will tell you things to come. He will glorify Me, for He will take of what is Mine and declare it to you" (John 16:13-14). A little later Jesus added, "And in that day you will ask Me nothing. Most assuredly, I say to you, whatever you ask the Father in My name He will give you. Until now you have asked nothing in My name. Ask and you will receive, that your joy may be full" (John 16:23-24).

Prayer, then, involves listening for God's guidance about our actions and even about what we should pray for, as much as it involves talking with God. But it's also a discipline that takes time and practice to learn well. The Psalms, because they are almost all prayers, can be great examples for us to follow in prayer, and that's one reason so many people make repeated reading of the Psalms a large part of their Bible reading. You can also get some help in developing a strong prayer life by reading Dallas Willard's *In Search of Guidance* (Ventura, CA: Regal Books, 1984), which will help you not only in prayer itself but also in learning to recognize God's guidance in your life. Other books that can help you in prayer include Warren and Ruth Myers's *Pray: How to Be Effective in Prayer* (Colorado Springs: NavPress, 1983), Brother Lawrence's short work *The Practice of the Presence of God* (Old Tappan, NJ: Revell, 1978), and A. W. Tozer's *The Pursuit of God* (Wheaton, IL: Tyndale House, n.d.).

As with Scripture memorization, finding a partner in prayer can be very helpful. Get together regularly—at least once a week, if possible. Some things you might pray about include: confessing your own sins (a good verse to memorize early is 1 John 1:9—"If we confess our sins, He is faithful and just to forgive us our sins and to cleanse us from all unrighteousness"), thanking God for giving you life in Christ, praising God for His goodness demonstrated in various blessings you experience, telling God your desires and asking Him to fulfill them, asking His guidance in thought and action, asking Him to take care of the needs of people you know, and asking for the salvation of non-Christian friends. The possibilities are endless. Essentially, whatever concerns you is a proper matter for prayer.

Often Bible reading, meditation, and study can be combined well with prayer during a specific time each day that you devote to meeting with God. Many Christians call this "devotions" or "quiet time." While nothing says this is absolutely necessary to the Christian life, most Christians find that when they are careful to set aside a certain time each day for attending to God and His Word, they grow spiritually and have a more clear and constant sense of God's presence, guidance, and peace. With this as with all other Christian practices—all things in life, in fact—it takes practice before we become completely comfortable and get the most benefit from it. Don't feel bad if your initial attempts seem dry and lifeless, or if those dry and lifeless periods come back from time to time; continued practice will result in increasingly fruitful times of Bible study and prayer.

Growing Through Obedience

"If anyone loves Me," Jesus said, "he will keep My word" (John 14:23). True love of God requires that we obey Him. As we learn to recognize His will through Bible study and prayer, we need also to do His will. As we do His will, we glorify Him and enjoy more and more intimate and profound communion, or friendship, with Him.

"I am the vine, you are the branches," Jesus said. "He who abides in Me, and I in him, bears much fruit; for without Me you can do nothing. If anyone does not abide in Me, he is cast out as a branch and is withered; and they gather them and throw them into the fire, and they are burned. If you abide in Me, and My words abide in you, you shall ask what you desire, and it shall be done for you. By this My Father is glorified, that you bear much fruit; so you will be My disciples. As the Father loved Me, I also have loved you; continue in My love. If you keep My commandments, you will abide in My love, just as I have kept My Father's commandments and abide in His love. These things I have spoken to you that My joy may remain in you, and that your joy may be full. This is My commandment, that you love one another as I have loved you. Greater love has no one than this, that he lay down his life for his friends.

You are My friends if you do whatever I command you" (John 15:5-14).

Obedience to Christ is one of the primary indicators of whether we truly believe in and love Him. This is why the Apostle James wrote, ". . . be doers of the word, and not hearers only, deceiving yourselves" (James 1:22). Here again, partnership is helpful. Having a Christian partner committed to helping you live an obedient life can mean the extra little motivation that sometimes makes the difference between obedience—with the blessing that comes with it—and disobedience, with its attendant sorrows.

This aspect of the Christian life, too, takes practice and patience. Remember that we have a fallen, sinful nature that continues to want to live in sin even after we have become Christians. That must be overcome by hard work with God's help if we are to become obedient and joyful. It's no wonder the Epistle to the Hebrews describes the spiritually mature as those who "by reason of use [literally, practice] have their senses exercised to discern both good and evil" (Hebrews 5:14). We'll never be perfect in this life, but we can grow in obedience to Christ. And when we fail, we can take comfort in the promise of 1 John 1:9—"If we confess our sins, He is faithful and just to forgive us our sins and to cleanse us from all unrighteousness."

Some books to help you grow in obedience are: Jerry Bridges's *The Pursuit of Holiness, The Practice of Godliness, Trusting God,* and *Transforming Grace* (Colorado Springs: NavPress, 1978, 1983, 1990, and 1992 respectively) and J. I. Packer's *I Want to Be a Christian* (Wheaton, IL: Tyndale House, 1977).

Growing Through Fellowship

"Two are better than one," wrote Solomon, "because they have a good reward for their labor. For if they fall, one will lift up his companion. But woe to him who is alone when he falls, for he has no one to help him up. Again, if two lie down together, they will keep warm; but how can one be warm alone? Though one may be overpowered by another, two can withstand him. And a threefold cord is not quickly broken" (Ecclesiastes 4:9-12).

This is one of the most important, but also one of the most neglected, principles of the Christian life. If we truly are to grow as Christians, we need the help of others who are committed to Christ and will commit themselves to helping us grow. And, because Christ teaches us that personal fulfillment comes in serving others, not in serving ourselves, real spiritual growth also requires that we invest ourselves in others—that we commit ourselves to helping them grow. We call this "fellowship" or, in more modern parlance, "partnership."

The early disciples met frequently together to grow as Christians. As Luke tells us, ". . . they continued steadfastly in the apostles' doctrine and fellowship, in the breaking of bread, and in prayers. And fear came upon every soul, and many wonders and signs were done through the apostles. And all who believed were together, and had all things in common, and sold their possessions and goods, and divided them among all, as anyone had need. And continuing daily with one accord in the temple, and breaking bread from house to house, they ate their food with gladness and simplicity of heart, praising God and having favor with all the people. And the Lord added to the church daily those who were being saved" (Acts 2:42-47).

Christians meet together for teaching, fellowship, sharing in the Lord's Supper—a special act Jesus instituted by which we commemorate His death for us—prayer, looking after each other's physical needs, and worship. As they do this, they grow stronger spiritually, and their lives become attractive to unbelievers. Each of the acts of the Christian life can be carried on alone and should also be carried on in the company of others, by which we can share our strength with them and receive strength back from them. This fellowship is especially important as a source of confidence, reassurance, and strength in the face of the daily difficulties of the Christian life, for through it we gain great encouragement. This is why we read, "Let us hold fast the confession of our hope without wavering, for He who promised is faithful. And let us consider one another so as to stir up love and good works, not forsaking the assembling of ourselves together, as is the manner of some, but exhorting one another, and so much the more as you see the Day approaching" (Hebrews 10:23-25). Encouraging each other in the faith and stimulating one another to "love and good deeds" are best done in company with other committed Christians, and they are essential to growth as Christians.

God has so designed Christians that when we come together in obedience to His will, we naturally build each other up. He has given different ones special skills and aptitudes that enable us to contribute in special ways to each other. As Paul put it, God ". . . gave some to be apostles, some prophets, some evangelists, and some pastors and teachers, for the perfecting of the saints for the work of ministry, for the edifying of the body of Christ, till we all come to the unity of the faith and the knowledge of the Son of God, to a perfect man, to the measure of the stature of the fullness of Christ; that we should no longer be children, tossed to and fro and carried about with every wind of doctrine, by the trickery of men, in the cunning craftiness by which they lie in wait to deceive, but, speaking the truth in love, may grow up in all things into Him who is the head— Christ—from whom the whole body, joined and knit together by what every joint supplies, according to the effective working by which every part does its share, causes growth of the body for the edifying of itself in love" (Ephesians 4:11-16).

It is important that you begin looking for a church congregation in which you can have fellowship, serving others and being served, where the pastor preaches clearly from the Bible and the members are committed to the vision of the church that Paul describes. Gene Getz's two books, *Building Up One Another* and *Loving One Another* (Wheaton, IL: Victor, both 1980), can help you understand how you and many other Christians can love and serve each other effectively. You may also find Bill Hull's *Jesus Christ Disciplemaker* (Colorado Springs: NavPress, 1984) helpful in understanding both how you can grow and how you can help others grow.

Growing Through Witnessing

Early in Christ's ministry, two men—one named Andrew—began following Him. Shortly after Andrew began following Him, he found his brother Simon and said, "We have found the Messiah." Then Andrew brought Simon to Jesus, and Simon became one of His followers. The next thing we read is that Philip, another follower of Jesus, "found Nathanael and said to him, 'We have found Him of whom Moses in the law, and also the prophets, wrote—Jesus of Nazareth, the son of Joseph,'" and Nathanael, too, became a follower of Jesus (John 1:41-49).

These early followers of Jesus were doing what comes naturally to someone who is excited about a new discovery. They were telling their relatives and friends about it. The Bible calls this "witnessing"—bearing testimony to what one has discovered or observed.

Witnessing is an important part of the Christian life. After His resurrection, Jesus told His disciples, "All authority has been given to Me in heaven and on earth. Go therefore and make disciples of all nations, baptizing them in the name of the Father and of the Son and of the Holy Spirit, teaching them to observe all things whatever I have commanded you; and behold, I am with you always, even to the end of the age"

(Matthew 28:18-20). But Jesus does not ask us to witness in our own power. Rather, He sends the Holy Spirit into us to give us power to witness effectively. Shortly before He ascended into Heaven, He said, ". . . you will receive power when the Holy Spirit has come upon you; and you will be witnesses to Me in Jerusalem, and in all Judea and Samaria, and to the end of the earth" (Acts 1:8).

The person who truly appreciates forgiveness of sin, is grateful to God for empowering him to triumph over sin, and looks forward eagerly to spending eternity—beginning now—in friendship with God will naturally want to share these things with others. His sharing will encourage him in his Christian walk as he sees others set free from sin and death.

Again, partnership helps. Two Christians can encourage each other and help discipline each other to share Christ frequently. Indeed, they can effectively witness together much of the time, each supporting what the other has to say, each praying quietly while the other speaks, each offering his own special insights to the inquiring listener. You can also get help in sharing Christ from Billy Graham's *How to Be Born Again* (Waco, TX: Word, 1977), Robert E. Coleman's *The Master Plan of Evangelism* (Old Tappan, NJ: Revell, 1984), and Jim Petersen's *Evangelism as a Lifestyle* (Colorado Springs: NavPress, 1980).

Growing With Jesus

"If then you were raised with Christ," Paul wrote to a congregation of Christians, "seek those things which are above, where Christ is, sitting at the right hand of God. Set your mind on things above, not on things on the earth. For you died, and your life is hidden with Christ in God" (Colossians 3:1-3). The center—the focus—of every Christian's life should be Jesus

Christ Himself. No one else should usurp that position, since Jesus Christ is our Creator, Sustainer, and Redeemer.

It was this attitude that enabled Paul to write, "I have been crucified with Christ; it is no longer I who live, but Christ lives in me; and the life which I now live in the flesh I live by faith in the Son of God, who loved me and gave Himself for me" (Galatians 2:20)—an excellent verse for early memorization.

"I am the true vine, and My Father is the vine-dresser," said Jesus. "Every branch in Me that does not bear fruit He takes away; and every branch that bears fruit He prunes, that it may bear more fruit. . . . Abide in Me, and I in you. As the branch cannot bear fruit of itself, unless it abides in the vine, neither can you, unless you abide in Me. I am the vine, you are the branches. He who abides in Me, and I in him, bears much fruit; for without Me you can do nothing" (John 15:1-2, 4-5). In everything that we think, feel, say, and do, we are to focus on Jesus and consider how He wants us to think, feel, speak, and act.

Nothing can be more exciting than getting to know Jesus better and better. Paul described Him as the One "in whom are hidden all the treasures of wisdom and knowledge" (Colossians 2:3). He is "the brightness of [God's] glory and the express image of His person" (Hebrews 1:3). We can know Christ better and better as we spend time studying His Word, praying, fellowshiping with other Christians, and telling others about Him. Ask Him to fill you with Himself and to show you the greatness of His glory, and He will respond!

Two books that can help you in this are St. Francis de Sales's *Introduction to the Devout Life* (Garden City, NY: Doubleday, 1972) and John Calvin's *Golden Booklet of the True Christian Life* (Grand Rapids, MI: Baker, 1977). Another helpful tool is *Discipleship Journal*, a bimonthly magazine published by The Navigators, designed to help Christians grow in knowing, following, and obeying Jesus. It contains articles that help people apply the Bible to their lives and includes Bible studies that help readers grapple with the Biblical text for themselves. Subscriptions may be ordered by writing to *Discipleship Journal*, Subscription Services, P.O. Box 6000, Colorado Springs, Colorado, 80934.

Appendix

Recommended Reading on Reasons for Faith and the Development of a Christian Worldview

General Apologetics

Anderson, Norman (J. N. D.). *A Lawyer Among the Theologians*. Grand Rapids, MI: Eerdmans, 1973. Applies principles of legal evidence to questions regarding the truth of Christianity; offers persuasive answers to anti-Christian and liberal "Christian" arguments.

Brown, Colin, ed. *History, Criticism, and Faith: Four Exploratory Studies*. Downers Grove, IL: InterVarsity Press, 1976. Essays by Gordon Wenham on Old Testament history and the reliability of the Old Testament; F. F. Bruce on New Testament history and the reliability of the New Testament; and Brown on the philosophy of history.

Carnell, Edward John. *An Introduction to Christian Apologetics: A Philosophic Defense of the Trinitarian-Theistic Faith*. Grand Rapids, MI: Eerdmans, 1950. One of the more important works in apologetics in this century; strongly influenced many contemporary apologists. Develops and defends a combinationalist approach to apologetics—i.e., combining historical and scientific evidences, philosophical arguments, and Biblical revelation.

Geisler, Norman L. *Christian Apologetics*. Grand Rapids, MI: Baker, 1976. An excellent philosophical approach to apologetics from the Thomistic perspective; contains very strong versions of the theistic arguments. Not as good, though, as his *Philosophy of Religion* (listed under *Philosophy* below).

Haley, John W. *An Examination of the Alleged Discrepancies of the Bible*. Nashville: Gospel Advocate Company, 1974 (rpt. of 1874 original). Tired of people telling you the Bible is full of contradictions? They've all been answered time and again for centuries. This is one of the best books on the subject. Next time you hear the charge, say, "Name one," and then whip out Haley, look up the text, and find the answer. The introduction alone, in which Haley explains how to deal with these problems, is worth the price of the book.

Henry, Carl F. H. *Toward a Recovery of Christian Belief*. Wheaton, IL: Crossway Books, 1990. An excellent argument for the primacy of Christian belief in rational thought.

Lewis, C. S. *Mere Christianity*. New York: Macmillan, 1960. A classic exposition and defense of the essentials of Christian faith. Profound, yet easy to understand.

——. *Miracles: A Preliminary Study*. New York: Macmillan, 1975. Answers arguments against the possibility of miracles and restores them to their reasonable place as part of God's way with man. Compelling reading, brilliant arguments.

——. *The Problem of Pain: The Intellectual Problem Raised by Human Suffering, Examined with Sympathy and Realism*. New York: Macmillan, 1976. Reasonably, persuasively, and sensitively answers the question, "If God is all-good and all-powerful and all-wise, then why is there evil?"

McDowell, Josh. *Evidence That Demands a Verdict: Historical Evidences for the Christian Faith.* San Bernardino, CA: Here's Life, 1972 (and many reprints). An excellent compendium of historical evidences but lacking in philosophical sophistication. Best used in combination with something like Lewis's *Mere Christianity*, Geisler's *Christian Apologetics*, or Carnell's *Introduction to Christian Apologetics*. Very persuasive with college students.

Montgomery, John Warwick. *Faith Founded on Fact: Essays in Evidential Apologetics.* Nashville: Thomas Nelson, 1978. Defends the use of evidences in defense of the faith and demonstrates how this can be done.

_____, ed. *Christianity for the Tough Minded.* Minneapolis: Bethany Fellowship, 1973. Contains good, clear answers to many of the questions that most plague university students and stand in the way of their embracing Christianity.

_____, ed. *Myth, Allegory, and Gospel: An Interpretation of J. R. R. Tolkien, C. S. Lewis, G. K. Chesterton, Charles Williams.* Minneapolis: Bethany Fellowship, 1974. See how these authors used the great archetypal themes of folk literature and mythology to communicate and defend the Christian faith. A fascinating book.

Moreland, J. P. *Scaling the Secular City: A Defense of Christianity.* Grand Rapids, MI: Baker, 1987. A good, fairly sophisticated philosophical defense of Christianity; particularly strong on the philosophy of science.

Orr, James. *The Christian View of God and the World.* Grand Rapids, MI: Kregel, 1989.

Plantinga, Alvin C. *God, Freedom, and Evil.* Grand Rapids, MI: Eerdmans, 1977. An excellent book on the problem of evil, the consistency of human freedom with divine foreknowledge and sovereignty, and three chief arguments for the existence of God: the cosmological argument (from the contingency of the universe), the teleological argument (from the fact of design in the universe), and the ontological argument (from the necessity of the existence of a perfect being). Sophisticated philosophy but possible for laymen to understand.

Plantinga, Theodore. *Learning to Live with Evil.* Grand Rapids, MI: Eerdmans, 1982. A good book answering the problem of evil; particularly helpful in that it puts the emphasis where it belongs: on the glory of God rather than on the wants of His creatures.

Smith, Wilbur M. *Therefore Stand: Christian Apologetics.* Grand Rapids, MI: Baker, 1976. A good overall survey of various methods and lines of Christian apologetics.

Van Til, Cornelius. *The Defense of the Faith.* Philadelphia: Presbyterian and Reformed, 1976. Lays out the presuppositional system of apologetics in its most systematic form and defends it against various criticisms.

Varghese, Roy Abraham. *The Intellectuals Speak Out About God.* Dallas: Lewis & Stanley, 1984. A stunning compilation of short essays by a long list of major intellectuals from a wide variety of fields, all in defense of theism. Particularly handy in witnessing to college students.

Wenham, John W. *The Goodness of God.* Downers Grove, IL: InterVarsity Press, 1974. A defense of the goodness of God in the face of the argument from evil in friendly, easy-to-understand style; generally rooted in the Bible.

The Bible—Introduction and Criticism

Archer, Gleason L., Jr. *A Survey of Old Testament Introduction.* Chicago: Moody Press, 1974. An excellent introduction to the Old Testament and response to various attacks on it by liberal (and not-so-liberal) writers.

Bruce, F. F. *The New Testament Documents: Are They Reliable?*, 5th ed. Downers Grove, IL: InterVarsity Press, 1974. Well, are they? Here's solid historical evidence.

Geisler, Norman L. and William E. Nix. *A General Introduction to the Bible.* Chicago: Moody Press, 1977. Defends the inspiration of the Bible; explains how the early Church recognized what books should be included and how the Bible was preserved and transmitted through the ages.

Guthrie, Donald. *New Testament Introduction,* 3rd ed. Downers Grove, IL: InterVarsity Press, 1970. Discusses authorship, date, purpose, theme, authenticity, and so on of every New Testament book; thoroughly decimates liberal critical views of New Testament books.

Harrison, R. K. *Introduction to the Old Testament, with a Comprehensive Review of Old Testament Studies and a Special Supplement on the Apocrypha.* Grand Rapids, MI: Eerdmans, 1974. Does for the Old Testament what Guthrie's does for the New, and then some.

Hodge, Archibald A. and Benjamin B. Warfield. *Inspiration.* Introduction by Roger R. Nicole. Grand Rapids, MI: Baker, 1979. Explains why Christians believe the Bible is God's Word, and what that implies.

Montgomery, John Warwick. *Crisis in Lutheran Theology,* 2 vols. Minneapolis: Bethany Fellowship, 1973. Intellectually rigorous answers to the toughest arguments against the inspiration of the Bible.

_____, ed. *God's Inerrant Word: An International Symposium on the Trustworthiness of Scripture.* Minneapolis: Bethany Fellowship, 1974. The best non-technical book in defense of the inspiration and inerrancy of Scripture.

Robinson, John A. T. *Redating the New Testament.* Philadelphia: Westminster Press, 1976. Liberal scholars claim most or all New Testament books were written long after the apostles died and are historically unreliable; here's historical argument that they were all written well within the lives of their claimed authors (all before A.D. 70, in fact) and are very reliable. And the book is by a very liberal theologian!

Comparative Religions

Anderson, J. N. D. *Christianity and Comparative Religion.* Downers Grove, IL: InterVarsity Press, 1977. Demonstrates the uniqueness of Christianity and its epistemological preferability compared with all other religions.

———, ed. *The World's Religions*, 4th ed. Grand Rapids, MI: Eerdmans, 1975. A good introductory survey and critique of the world's major religions from an evangelical perspective.

Martin, Walter. *The Kingdom of the Cults*, rev. ed. Minneapolis: Bethany Fellowship, 1985. The best survey and analysis of the various major pseudo-Christian cults in America.

———, ed. *The New Cults.* Ventura, CA: Vision House, 1983. The best survey and critique of various new pseudo-Christian cults in America.

Miller, Elliot. *A Crash Course on the New Age Movement: Describing and Evaluating a Growing Social Force.* Grand Rapids, MI: Baker, 1989. Some earlier books (particularly those by Texe Marrs, Dave Hunt, and Constance Cumbey) have been more popular and sensational, but this is far and away the most reliable, scholarly, and perceptive analysis of the New Age Movement yet published; and the author is a former New Ager.

Miller, William M. *A Christian's Response to Islam.* Nutley, NJ: Presbyterian and Reformed, 1976. Islam is the fastest-growing religion in the world today (with the possible exception of Christianity), largely because the Muslims are not falling for the anti-natalist propaganda of the population scare people. Islam is also the biggest challenge facing Christianity in the next century. It is vital that we know how to answer its followers. This book provides excellent help. Clearly written, by a true expert on Islam, a missionary to Iran for forty-three years and an expert on Islamic law.

Passantino, Bob and Gretchen. *Answers to the Cultist at Your Door.* Eugene, OR: Harvest House, 1978. No book better explains how to communicate to people involved in or hurt by the cults and other religions. This is warm, friendly, easy to understand, and easy to use.

History—Biblical and Ecclesiastical

Albright, William Foxwell. *From the Stone Age to Christianity: Monotheism and the Historical Process.* Garden City, NY: Doubleday/Anchor, 1957. Excellent source for ancient Near Eastern history, founded on outstanding archaeological studies. Albright, though not a Christian, argued strongly for the historical reliability of the Old Testament.

Bruce, F. F. *Jesus and Christian Origins Outside the New Testament.* Grand Rapids: Eerdmans, 1974. The New Testament isn't our only source of information about Jesus and early Christianity. Other early sources confirm what we find in it.

_____. *New Testament History.* Garden City, NY: Doubleday/ Anchor, 1972. An outstanding guide to the events of Christianity during the Apostolic Age. Well written, easy to read.

_____. *The Spreading Flame: The Rise and Progress of Christianity from John the Baptist to the Conversion of the English.* Exeter, England: Paternoster Press, 1976. An exciting story!

Latourette, Kenneth Scott. *A History of Christianity*, rev. ed., 2 vols. New York: Harper and Row, 1975. An outstanding, comprehensive, layman's-level survey of the whole of Church history. Well written and entertaining.

Lindsay, Thomas M. *A History of the Reformation*, 2nd ed., 2 vols. Edinburgh, Scotland: T. & T. Clark, 1963. Among many histories of the Reformation, this is one of the most reliable, exciting, and useful for understanding the theological controversies.

Pfeiffer, Charles F. *Old Testament History*. Grand Rapids, MI: Baker, 1973. If you have trouble keeping all the kings and prophets in their proper historical settings, this book will be of great help. It's nearly impossible to understand the prophets, in particular, if we don't have them properly placed in historical context.

Schaff, Philip. *History of the Christian Church*, 8 vols. Grand Rapids, MI: Eerdmans, 1960. The most thorough and reliable study of Church history from the Apostolic Age through the Reformation.

Sheldon, Henry C. *History of the Christian Church*, 5 vols. Peabody, MA: Hendrickson Publishers, 1988. Particularly for post-Reformation history, this is a great supplement to Schaff.

Vos, Howard F. *Beginnings in Bible Archaeology*. Chicago: Moody Press, 1973. An excellent little book to get started in studying Bible archeology.

———. *Beginnings in Church History*. Chicago: Moody Press, 1977. Does the same as the previous book, but for Church history.

Logic

Copi, Irving M. *Introduction to Logic*, 4th ed. New York: Macmillan, 1972. Through the years this remains one of the best textbooks on logic. Study it carefully and you'll rarely be fooled by any illogical argument, whether its fallacies are formal or informal.

Emmet, E. R. *Handbook of Logic*. Totowa, NJ: Littlefield, Adams, 1981. A helpful refresher course.

Geisler, Norman L. and Ronald Brooks. *Come Let Us Reason Together: An Introduction to Logic*. Grand Rapids, MI: Baker, 1990. Logic is the same for everybody, Christian or non-

Christian, but this book does a good job of making lots of difficult concepts clear and of using illustrations that are particularly helpful to Christians concerned about making sure they can give good reasons for faith or sound arguments for their theological positions.

Fischer, David Hackett. *Historians' Fallacies: Toward a Logic of Historical Thought.* New York: Harper/Colophon Books, 1970. A witty, entertaining, challenging, very instructive look at how historians often commit logical fallacies, how they can avoid them, and how all of us can become more careful in our thinking about history and everything else.

Weinland, James D. *How to Think Straight.* Totowa, NJ: Littlefield, Adams, 1980. A very helpful book of practical, easy-to-use rules for sensible thinking. (But beware of Weinland's own logical slip-ups, particularly those rooted in his antisupernaturalistic presuppositions.)

Philosophy

Barclay, Oliver R. *The Intellect and Beyond: Developing a Christian Mind.* Grand Rapids, MI: Zondervan/Academie Books, 1985. A creative, thoughtful, enjoyable book that is particularly strong on how to use the Bible to develop a Christian mind.

Blamires, Harry. *The Christian Mind: How Should a Christian Think?* Ann Arbor, MI: Servant Books, 1963. A good rudimentary study of how to develop a Christian worldview and thought process.

Brown, Colin. *Philosophy and the Christian Faith.* Downers Grove, IL: InterVarsity Press, 1978. A good historical survey of various philosophies and philosophers, always assessing them by Christian faith and revelation.

Custance, Arthur C. *The Mysterious Matter of Mind.* Grand Rapids, MI: Zondervan/Probe Ministries/Christian Free University Curriculum, 1980. An excellent book on the

Christian position regarding the mind/body problem; argues persuasively that the mind cannot be explained on materialist grounds.

Flint, Robert. *Theism: Being the Baird Lecture for 1876*, 8th ed. New York: Charles Scribner's Sons, 1912. One of the outstanding philosophical defenses of theism of all time. Thorough and persuasive answers to all the major antitheistic arguments and arguments for alternatives to theism (pantheism, atheism, agnosticism, polytheism, etc.).

Geehan, E. R., ed. *Jerusalem and Athens: Critical Discussions on the Philosophy and Apologetics of Cornelius Van Til.* Nutley, NJ: Presbyterian and Reformed, 1977. An excellent collection of essays criticizing and defending the presuppositionalist apologetic theory of Cornelius Van Til. Presuppositionalism has become increasingly important in recent years, and understanding it and knowing where we stand regarding it is important for any Christian involved in apologetics.

Geisler, Norman L. *Philosophy of Religion.* Grand Rapids, MI: Zondervan, 1974. This is an outstanding work in which Geisler is at his best. Various theistic arguments and answers to the problem of evil receive some of their best treatment in this volume. Heavy going but well worth it. Geisler works from a Thomistic perspective.

Gill, Jerry H. *The Possibility of Religious Knowledge.* Grand Rapids, MI: Eerdmans, 1971. A sound basic defense of religious knowledge.

Hume, David. *Dialogues Concerning Natural Religion.* New York: Macmillan/Hafner Press, 1975 (and many other editions). Read this carefully and see why some of the best Christian philosophers believe Hume actually revealed here that he was a Christian out to debunk anti-Christian arguments and at the same time to warn fellow Christians of the weaknesses in many traditional arguments.

Hunnex, Milton D. *Existentialism and Christian Belief: A Frank Appraisal of a Modern-day Philosophy*. Chicago: Moody Press, 1972. A good critique of existentialism; easy to understand, yet sophisticated enough to handle the various arguments pro and con. Helpful to college students stuck with professors of existentialist philosophy (or literature, or art, or political science, or anything else) who are trying to proselytize for their faith.

Plantinga, Alvin. *The Nature of Necessity*. Oxford, England: Oxford University Press, 1974. A tremendous defense of a classical Christian metaphysical worldview and epistemology, capped by a compelling theodicy (answer to the problem of evil). If you haven't fairly mastered logic yet, you might do well to do that before reading this book.

Rushdoony, Rousas John. *The One and the Many: Studies in the Philosophy of Order and Ultimacy*. Nutley, NJ: Craig Press, 1971. A powerful and insightful study of how Christianity's answer to the philosophical problem of the one and the many, an answer provided by the doctrine of the Trinity ("Which is ultimate, unity or plurality? Both!"), provides the basis for the ordering of Western civilization that preserves us from both tyranny and anarchy. Unfortunately, Enlightenment thinking has attacked that foundation, and hundreds of millions of people have lived under tyranny and anarchy because of that.

Spier, J. M. *An Introduction to Christian Philosophy*. Nutley, NJ: Craig Press, 1976. A good survey/introduction.

Trueblood, D. Elton. *Philosophy of Religion*. Grand Rapids, MI: Baker, 1977. An excellent work from a classical perspective in defense of Christian belief.

Willard, Dallas. *Logic and the Objectivity of Knowledge: A Study in Husserl's Early Philosophy*. Athens, OH: Ohio University Press, 1984. Probably one of the finest defenses of Christian realist metaphysics and epistemology.

Young, Warren C. *A Christian Approach to Philosophy*. Grand Rapids, MI: Baker, 1975. A good introduction to the subject for beginners (though it is not simplistic or superficial).

Science

Anderson, J. Kerby and Harold G. Coffin. *Fossils in Focus*. Grand Rapids, MI: Zondervan/Probe Ministries/Christian Free University Curriculum, 1977. A very good book showing why the fossil record is inconsistent with the theory of macro-evolution; by authors with credentials in evolutionary biology and paleontology. Short and readily understandable.

Beveridge, W. I. B. *The Art of Scientific Investigation*. New York: Random House/Vintage Books, no date. Ever heard of the "scientific method"? Ever heard there isn't any such thing? Here's an excellent book on how scientists work, one that dispels myths of perfect objectivity and instead reveals how much science is an art. The book is not designed to support creationism.

Bird, W. R. *The Origin of Species Revisited: The Theories of Evolution and of Abrupt Appearance*, 2 vols. New York: The Philosophical Library, 1989. The most impressive, magnificently documented study of the evolution/creation controversy I've seen. Covers philosophy of science, nature of scientific evidence, scientific methodology, philosophy of religion, epistemological relationship between science and religion, wide variety of evidences claimed for both evolution and creation, constitutional issues, pedagogical issues, academic freedom issues, and lots more. If you read this, you'll know more about the evolution/creation controversy than all but a handful of people in the world.

Frair, Wayne and P. William Davis. *The Case for Creation: An Evaluation of Modern Evolutionary Thought from a Biblical*

Perspective. Chicago: Moody Press, 1976. Frair and Davis are both bona fide biologists, and their book is very persuasive and easy to understand.

Macbeth, Norman. *Darwin Retried: An Appeal to Reason: How Modern Science Not Only Fails to Confirm Darwinian Theory But Finds New Mystery in the Course of Evolution.* Ipswich, MA: Gambit, 1971. Macbeth doesn't reject the overall scheme of evolution, but he sure pokes holes in practically all the evidentiary claims for it, showing especially where pro-evolution scientists violate rules of logic, play fast and loose with evidence, ignore contrary evidence, and so on. A very useful book.

Moreland, J. P. *Christianity and the Nature of Science: A Philosophical Investigation.* Grand Rapids, MI: Baker, 1989. Shows that popular notions (shared by most working scientists and by almost all college, secondary, and primary-level science teachers) of the nature and methods of science are far from what the great scientists do and have done and far from what great scientists and philosophers have always thought science is and does. Then it shows convincingly that creationism is truly scientific on any standard of measurement. An outstanding book that deserves thorough reading.

Morris, Henry M., *et al.,* eds. *Scientific Creationism.* El Cajon, CA: Master Books, 1974. Probably the best introductory study of evidences for creation, but the arguments often are so oversimplified as to be unpersuasive to many people who are reasonably sophisticated in science. After this introduction, go to Bird, Wilder-Smith, and Moreland.

Polanyi, Michael. *Science, Faith, and Society: A Searching Examination of the Meaning and Nature of Scientific Inquiry.* Chicago: University of Chicago Press, 1964. One of the books that have exploded the myth of the "scientific method," of positivistic science, of scientific objectivity. Polanyi's authority as a physical chemist and social scientist is unchallenged in the secular world.

Whitcomb, John C., Jr., and Henry M. Morris. *The Genesis Flood: The Biblical Record and Its Scientific Implications.* Grand Rapids, MI: Baker, 1974. A monumental work majoring on geological evidences against evolution and for a young earth and the universal flood.

Wilder-Smith, A. E. *Man's Origin, Man's Destiny: A Critical Survey of the Principles of Evolution and Christianity.* Minneapolis: Bethany Fellowship, 1975. Arguments against evolution from organic chemistry. Persuasive.

Social Issues and Sociology

Kirk, Russell. *Enemies of the Permanent Things: Observations of Abnormity in Literature and Politics.* LaSalle, IL: Sherwood Sugden & Company, 1984. A masterful critique of the ideologies and trends that threaten to destroy Western civilization.

Olasky, Marvin. *Prodigal Press: The Anti-Christian Bias of the American News Media.* Wheaton, IL: Crossway Books, 1988. Not just a protest, but also a fine positive prescription for how Christians can reshape journalism and broadcast media news.

Peacocke, Dennis. *Winning the Battle for the Minds of Men.* Santa Rosa, CA: Alive & Free, 1987. Written by a former radical Marxist of Berkeley's 1960s glory days; it will encourage you to go out and change the way people think, to bring all thoughts captive to Christ.

Schlossberg, Herbert. *Idols For Destruction: Christian Faith and Its Confrontation with American Society.* Nashville: Thomas Nelson, 1983. One of the most important Christian books published in the 1980s. It woke up scores of Christian leaders to the need to confront our culture with sound Biblical and reasonable critique and with prescriptions for cure. One of the best books available for developing a well-rounded Christian worldview.

Theology

Bavinck, Herman. *The Doctrine of God*. Translated by William Hendriksen. Grand Rapids, MI: Baker, 1977. A clear, scholarly, compelling study of the nature of God; solidly Biblical.

Berkhof, Louis. *The History of Christian Doctrines*. Carlisle, PA: Banner of Truth Trust, 1975. An excellent brief survey of the subject; helpful to anyone who wants to know the basics of what has always defined Christianity and set it off from heresy and non-Christianity.

Calvin, John. *Institutes of the Christian Religion*, 2 vols. Translated by Ford Lewis Battles; edited by John T. McNeill. Philadelphia: Westminster Press, 1977. One of the true classics of the whole history of Christianity; a great survey of all the major beliefs, disciplines, and ethics of the Christian faith.

Charnock, Stephen. *The Existence and Attributes of God*, 2 vols. Grand Rapids, MI: Baker, 1979. The finest study of the nature and attributes of God ever; marvelous devotional reading, stuff that will break your heart and lift your spirit in praise and in a longing for holiness.

Harrison, Everett F., Geoffrey W. Bromiley, and Carl F. H. Henry, eds. *Baker's Dictionary of Theology*. Grand Rapids, MI: Baker, 1975. Precisely what it says it is; excellent.

MacArthur, John F., Jr. *The Gospel According to Jesus*. Grand Rapids, MI: Zondervan, 1988. Soundly refutes the notion that one can have Jesus as Savior without submitting to Him as Lord; tells what becoming a Christian really means and what difference it makes in one's life.

Morris, Leon. *The Apostolic Preaching of the Cross*. Grand Rapids, MI: Eerdmans, 1976. A masterful study of the doctrine of the atonement, one of the most important doctrines in Christianity, as preached by the apostles and taught in the New Testament.

Schaff, Philip. *The Creeds of Christendom*, 3 vols. Grand Rapids, MI: Baker, 1977. It is essential that we know, or at least have access to, the doctrinal standards that undergird the Christian churches. These provide that access.

Worldview Development

Jordan, James B. *Through New Eyes: Developing a Biblical View of the World.* Brentwood, TN: Wolgemuth & Hyatt, 1988. A fascinating, challenging, refreshing discussion of how the Bible views man and the world under God, with excellent discussions of ethics, aesthetics, art, music, economic value, and a wide variety of other subjects.

Henry, Carl F. H. *The Christian Mindset in a Secular Society: Promoting Evangelical Renewal and National Righteousness.* Portland, OR: Multnomah Press, 1984. The essays on religious freedom and modern learning are particularly worthwhile.

Lewis, C. S. *The Discarded Image: An Introduction to Medieval and Renaissance Literature.* Cambridge, England: Cambridge University Press, 1976. See how the Christian worldview shaped the thinking of the writers of these periods, and learn how it can help us regain a sense of the wonder and mystery of God's creation. A fascinating book.

Morris, Lynne, ed. *The Christian Vision: Man in Society.* Hillsdale, MI: Hillsdale College Press, 1984. Outstanding essays by Thomas Burke (on Christian studies and liberal arts), Carl F. H. Henry (on the crisis in modern learning), Thomas Howard (on mere Christianity, a focus on man in society), Stanley L. Jaki ("God and Man's Science: A View of Creation"), Gerhart Niemeyer ("Augustine's Political Philosophy?"), Paul C. Vitz ("A Covenant Theory of Personality: A Theoretical Introduction"), and J. I. Packer ("A Christian View of Man").

Noebel, David A. *Understanding the Times: The Story of the Biblical Christian, Marxist/Leninist, and Secular Humanist Worldviews.*

Manitou Springs, CO: Summit Press, 1991. A tremendous work of comparative presentation and analysis; fairly represents the chief competing modern worldviews; argues persuasively in the conclusion for Christianity. Includes excellent appendix on the New Age worldview.

Schaeffer, Francis A. *The Complete Works of Francis A. Schaeffer: A Christian Worldview*, 5 vols. Vol. 1: *A Christian View of Philosophy and Culture*; Vol. 2: *A Christian View of the Bible as Truth*; Vol. 3: *A Christian View of Spirituality*; Vol. 4: *A Christian View of the Church*; Vol. 5: *A Christian View of the West*. Wheaton, IL: Crossway Books, 1982. There could hardly be a finer way to get started in understanding the Christian worldview than to read all of these books by Schaeffer.

About the Author

E. Calvin Beisner is a writer, editor, and speaker on Christian apologetics, worldview, ethics, and the application of Christian theology to economics, political science, and public policy. A visiting lecturer in interdisciplinary studies at Covenant College, atop Lookout Mountain, Georgia, he is the author of seven books and over one hundred published articles and book reviews, technical and popular, and a contributor to several books. He has been an interview guest on national radio and television programs and speaks widely for Christian college, school, and church audiences. He is among the founding members of The Coalition on Revival and is the national chairman of its economics committee. He has been a newspaper and magazine reporter, editor, and publisher and is an elder in the Presbyterian Church in America. He and his wife Deborah live in an old house in the historic St. Elmo district of Chattanooga, Tennessee, with their five children—David, Susan, Kilby, Becky, and Peter.

For information about writing, editing, and speaking services or to request order forms for books, articles, or lectures (transcript or computer disk), contact:

E. Calvin Beisner, 4409 Alabama Avenue, Chattanooga, Tennessee 37409.

Endnotes

1. Robert Jastrow, *God and the Astronomers* (New York: Warner Books, 1984), pp. 11-16.
2. See J. P. Moreland, *Christianity and the Nature of Science* (Grand Rapids, MI: Baker, 1989).
3. Translation adapted from the *King James Version*.
4. Flavius Josephus, *Antiquities of the Jews*, XVIII.iii.3. This is the wording of a tenth-century manuscript discovered in late 1971 or early 1972 and for the authenticity of which there is strong evidence, despite the existence of several alternative readings. For discussion, see *New York Times* press release, Feb. 12, 1972, published under the title "Christ Documentation: Israeli Scholars Find Ancient Document They Feel Confirms the Existence of Jesus"; *Palm Beach Post-Times,* Feb. 13, 1972; "Josephus and Jesus," *Time,* Feb. 28, 1972, p. 55. Cited in David A. Noebel, *Understanding the Times: The Story of the Biblical Christian, Marxist/Leninist, and Secular Humanist Worldviews* (Manitou Springs, CO: Summit Press, 1991), p. 772.
5. Cornelius Tacitus, *Annals* XV.44; cited in Noebel, p. 792.
6. For more references to Jesus outside the New Testament, see F. F. Bruce, *Jesus and Christian Origins Outside the New Testament* (Grand Rapids, MI: Eerdmans, 1974).
7. C. S. Lewis, *Mere Christianity* (London: Collins Fontana Books, 1960), pp. 52-3.
8. See F. F. Bruce, *The New Testament Documents: Are They Reliable?* (Grand Rapids, MI: Eerdmans, 1959) and *New Testament History* (Garden City, NY: Doubleday/Anchor Books, 1972); Jack Finegan, *Light From the Ancient Past* (Princeton, NJ: Princeton University Press, 1946); Sir

189

William M. Ramsay, *Pauline and Other Studies in Early Church History* (Grand Rapids, MI: Baker, 1979); Howard F. Vos, *Beginnings in Church History* (Chicago: Moody Press, 1977).

9.   See also Matthew 12:40; 16:4; 17:22-23; 23:32; Mark 9:9; 10:34; Luke 9:22, 31; 24:6-7.

10. For detailed evidences for the resurrection of Jesus, see Frank Morison, *Who Moved the Stone?* (Grand Rapids, MI: Zondervan, reprint, n.d.); Josh McDowell, *Evidence That Demands a Verdict* (San Bernardino, CA: Here's Life, 1972).

11. To study the Old Testament prophecies Jesus fulfilled, see J. Barton Payne, *Encyclopedia of Biblical Prophecy* (New York: Harper & Row, 1973), especially the list on pp. 665-70 and the detailed explanation of each passage throughout the book.

12. For more discussion of the meaning and truth of the doctrine of the Trinity, see E. Calvin Beisner, *God in Three Persons* (Wheaton, IL: Tyndale House, 1984).

13. This argument is adapted from R. C. Sproul, "The Case for Inerrancy: A Methodological Analysis," in *God's Inerrant Word*, ed. John Warwick Montgomery (Minneapolis: Bethany Fellowship, 1974), pp. 242-61.

14. Fred Hoyle and Chandra Wickramasinghe, *Evolution from Space: A Theory of Cosmic Creationism* (New York: Simon & Schuster, 1984). See also Fred Hoyle, *The Intelligent Universe: A New View of Creation and Evolution* (New York: Henry Holt, 1984).

15. Henry M. Morris, *Men of Science, Men of God*, rev. ed. (El Cajon, CA: Master Books, 1988).

16. Julian Huxley, *Evolution in Action* (New York: Harper & Brothers, 1953), p. 41. Other books that discuss the arguments pro and con on evolution include: J. Kerby Anderson and Harold G. Coffing, *Fossils in Focus* (Grand Rapids, MI: Zondervan/Probe, 1977; creationist); Niles Eldredge, *The Monkey Business* (New York: Washington Square Press, 1983; evolutionist); Wayne Frair and P. William Davis, *The Case for Creation* (Chicago: Moody Press, 1973; creationist); Carl F. H. Henry, ed., *Horizons of Science* (San Francisco: Harper & Row, 1978; contains two essays, by Richard Bube and Gareth Jones, offering theistic evolutionary views); Francis Hitching, *The Neck of the Giraffe: Where Darwin Went Wrong* (New York: Ticknor & Fields, 1982; assesses arguments pro and con and calls for further research and suspended judgments); Norman Macbeth, *Darwin Retried: An Appeal to Reason* (Ipswich, MA: Gambit, 1971; suspended judgment); Henry M. Morris, *et al.*, eds., *Scientific Creationism* (El Cajon, CA: Master Books; creationist); Michael Polanyi, *Science, Faith and Society* (Chicago: University of Chicago Press, 1964; analyzes relationships among science, faith, and society; argues that science and faith are not opposed); John C. Whitcomb, Jr. and Henry M. Morris, *The Genesis Flood* (Grand Rapids, MI: Baker, 1974; creationist); A. E. Wilder-Smith, *Man's Origin, Man's Destiny: A Critical*

Survey of the Principles of Evolution and Christianity (Minneapolis: Bethany Fellowship, 1974; creationist); R. J. Wilson, ed., *Darwinism and the American Intellectual* (Homewood, IL: Dorsey Press, 1967; analyzes social implications of evolutionary—particularly Darwinist—thought); Davis A. Young, *Christianity and the Age of the Earth* (Grand Rapids, MI: Zondervan, 1982; creationist); Wendell R. Bird, *The Origin of Species Revisited*, 2 vols. (New York: Philosophical Library, 1989; creationist).

17.   See J. P. Moreland, *Christianity and the Nature of Science: A Philosophical Investigation* (Grand Rapids, MI: Baker, 1989); Stanley L. Jaki, *The Origin of Science and the Science of Its Origin* (Washington, D.C.: Regnery Gateway, 1979), *The Road of Science and the Ways to God* (Chicago: University of Chicago Press, 1980), and *The Savior of Science* (Washington: Regnery Gateway, 1988).

18.   William F. Albright, *The Archaeology of Palestine* (Baltimore: Penguin Books, 1960). See also Finegan, *Light from the Ancient Past*; Norman L. Geisler and William E. Nix, *A General Introduction to the Bible* (Chicago: Moody Press, 1977); Werner Keller, *The Bible as History*, rev. ed. Joachim Rehork, eds. William Neil and B. H. Rasmussen (New York: Morrow, 1981); Kathleeen Kenyon, *The Bible and Recent Archaeology* (Atlanta: John Knox Press, 1979); McDowell, *Evidence That Demands a Verdict*; Howard F. Vos, *Beginnings in Bible Archaeology* and *Beginnings in Church History* (Chicago: Moody Press, 1973 and 1977).

19.   Geisler and Nix, *General Introduction to the Bible*, pp. 366-7.

20.   On the textual authenticity of the Bible, see Geisler and Nix, *General Introduction to the Bible*; McDowell, *Evidence That Demands a Verdict* and *More Evidence That Demands a Verdict* (San Bernardino, CA: Here's Life, 1975); Gleason Archer, *A Survey of Old Testament Introduction* (Chicago: Moody Press, 1974); F. F. Bruce, *The New Testament Documents: Are They Reliable?* (Downers Grove, IL: InterVarsity Press, 1974) and *The Books and the Parchments*, rev. ed. (Old Tappan, NJ: Revell, n.d.); J. Harold Greenlee, *Introduction to New Testament Textual Criticism* (Grand Rapids, MI: Eerdmans, 1980); Donald Guthrie, *New Testament Introduction* (Downers Grove, IL: InterVarsity Press, 1974); Roland K. Harrison, *Introduction to the Old Testament* (Grand Rapids, MI: Eerdmans, 1974); George Eldon Ladd, *The New Testament and Criticism* (Grand Rapids, MI: Eerdmans, 1967); Theodor Zahn, *Introduction to the New Testament*, 3 vols. (Minneapolis: Klock & Klock, 1953).

21.   Peter T. Bauer, *Dissent on Development* ([1971] 1976), *Equality, the Third World, and Economic Delusion* (1981), *Reality and Rhetoric: Studies in the Economics of Development* (1984) (Cambridge, MA: Harvard University Press), *Economic Analysis and Policy in Underdeveloped Countries* (Duke University Commonwealth-Studies Center Publication No. 4; Westport, CT: Greenwood Press, 1981), and *West African Trade* (New York: Augustus M. Kelley, 1967).